Classroom Organization and Management

Strategies for Establishing and
Maintaining an Effective
Learning Environment

Lisa Dellamora

Illustrated by Becky Radtke

Rigby Best Teachers Press®

An imprint of Rigby ®

To José, José, and the Pussycats

Kirsten "Hooch" Becker   *Colleen "Coll" Birnstiel*
Sarah "Riles" Riley   *Elizabeth "Lizlove" Lehre*
Michael "Tex" Ritter   *Julie "Jules" Golden*
Bob "Swimbobby" Allison   *Caroline "CC" Conley*

What would I do without you guys? Thanks for being there for me!
— Stella

Special thanks to Beverly and the teachers at PS315 in Brooklyn who helped inspire me to write a book like this.

For more information about other books from Rigby Best Teachers Press, please contact Rigby at 800-531-5015 or visit **www.rigby.com**

Editors: Amy Kinsman and Justine Dunn
Executive Editor: Georgine Cooper
Designer: Nancy Rudd
Design Production Manager: Tom Sjoerdsma
Cover Photographer: Sharon Hoogstraten
Interior Illustrator: Becky Radtke

Contents

Preface 4

Introduction 7

   General Beliefs About Children 7

   Building a Solid Foundation 8

   Effective Instruction Begins with Classroom
   Management 10

   Section Overviews 12

Section 1 Creating a Climate Conducive to Learning 13

Chapter 1: Organizing for Space 14

   How Does the Classroom Feel? 16

   How Does the Classroom Look? 19

   How Does the Classroom Sound? 32

Chapter 2: Organizing for Time 34

   Finding Time to Fit It all In 34

   Scheduling: Putting the Puzzle Pieces Together .. 36

   Creating More Minutes in the Day 39

Chapter 3: Organizing for Assessment 45

   Informal Assessment 46

   Formal Assessment 51

   Finding the Time 56

   Keeping Track of It All 56

Section 2 Setting the Tone for the Rest of the Year 58

Chapter 4: Establishing Ongoing Routines 59

   Rule vs. Expectation 59

   Organizing and Managing Your Classroom for
   Optimal Effectiveness: Ongoing Routines 62

Chapter 5: Putting It All Together for the First Weeks of School 74

   Before School Starts 74

   The First Day of School 75

   The First Week of School 77

   Weeks Two and Three 80

   Weeks Four and Five 82

   Week Six and Beyond 83

   Handling Challenging Behavior 84

Section 3 Managing Student Centers 90

Chapter 6: Management Systems 91

   Teacher-Led Management Systems 92

   Student-Directed Management Systems 96

Chapter 7: Organizing Centers with Engaging Activities 99

   Classroom Library 101

   Poetry Center 103

   Writing Center 106

   Handwriting/Penmanship Center 110

   Read the Room 111

   Art Center 113

   Word Zone 115

   Listening Center 119

Appendix 121

Bibliography 150

©2003 Rigby

Classroom Organization and Management: *Strategies for Establishing and Maintaining an Effective Learning Environment*   **3**

Preface

According to Harry Wong (1998) "What you do on the first days of school will determine your success or failure for the rest of the school year. You will either win or lose your class on the first day of school" (3).

One year, I nearly managed to lose my class on that first day. I would have spent the rest of the year fighting the very structure that I had established in the first place if it were not for a student I will call Miguel. I learn from children in my classroom on a daily basis, but what Miguel taught me about my responsibilities as a teacher during those first critical days of school are lessons I will never forget.

During the first week of school, Miguel and I experienced our first fire drill. My experience, training, and intuition told me to respond in a calm manner, knowing I would need to move my frightened and confused kindergarten students outside quickly in an orderly fashion. Miguel's response was to run from the classroom, arms flailing, screaming "FIRE!!!" at the top of his lungs.

In an instant, Miguel taught me the importance of being *proactive*. Following him through the hallway screaming and then admonishing him would have be a *reactive* response, resulting from my embarrassment in the reflection his behavior made on me as a teacher. Instead, I chose to realize that the fault for the situation was mine. Had I been wiser, I would have taken the opportunity in advance to explain to my students that fire drills were just that and not actual fires.

My solution was to round up my scattered students, apologize to the fire marshal and the principal, and then provide my students the leadership and direction they deserved by training them how to respond appropriately the next time we had a fire drill.

Steven Covey, author of the bestseller *The 7 Habits of Highly Effective People*, also taught me how to be proactive—only learning from Covey was a lot less embarrassing.

Covey (1989) describes proactivity as being "more than merely taking initiative. It means that as human beings, we are responsible for our own lives. Our behavior is a function of our decisions, not our conditions"… (71).

I can hear a similar message echoing through my mind as I mentally replay the scene from the movie *Dangerous Minds* (1995) when Michelle Pfeiffer repeatedly reminds her students "You have a choice!" They respond with an eternity of "but..."; however, she remains steadfast in insisting that no matter what the situation, there is *some* choice to be made. Whether the choice is in how you react to something or in how you let it affect you, you have a choice. You *always* have a choice.

Covey (1989) suggests that what you say and how you say it indicates the degree to which you are being proactive. In an academic setting, you can reflect on your words to self-evaluate your level of proactivity as an instructional leader.

Reactive Language	Proactive Language
• I always get the "bad" students.	• Let's see what I can do.
• That wouldn't work in *my* class.	• I'll try it.
• I have too many students in my class.	• I can try a different approach.
• He drives the other students crazy.	• I can help the other students learn how to respond.
• She drives me crazy.	• I will choose an appropriate response.
• The principal/fire marshal/district won't let me …	• I can control my own feelings.
• I have to …	• I prefer …
• I can't …	• I will …
• If only …	• I choose …

Adapted from *The 7 Habits of Highly Effective People* by Steven Covey © 1989 Simon and Schuster.

The problem with reactive language is that it can become a self-fulfilling prophecy (Covey 1989). Think how long my school year would have been if I had chosen to respond to Miguel reactively. If he had not helped me realize the importance of being proactive, I probably would have ended up following his suit and run screaming from the building, waving my arms as well. Maybe not that day, or the next, but I would not have lasted very long as a teacher.

Spend a week or so becoming aware of the statements you make in reference to your classroom responsibilities. Write them down as you catch yourself making them and sort them into two categories: Proactive and Reactive. This is the first step to establishing yourself as a more proactive teacher.

To hold, daily, in my hands the responsibility of affecting children in powerful and lasting ways is one of the greatest honors I ever have or will be privileged to receive. Education is a profession that brings a complex set of opportunities, challenges, and, ultimately, rewards to both the teacher and the learners. Teaching is an awesome task, to say the least.

This book is an offering to you of my vast research and collective experiences. The best practices for organizing and managing the classroom come from years of working with students in my own classroom as well as students in others' classrooms and leading countless teacher in-services across the country. As you read through this book, pick and choose the strategies that work best for you and your students to create your own classroom management plan.

Introduction

There is a well-known children's song that compares the choices of two men, one very wise and the other very foolish, who set out to build houses for themselves. The wise man built his house on the rock and the foolish man built his house on the sand. When the rains came down and the floods came rushing up, the house on the rock stood firm while the house on the sand collapsed. This song illustrates the importance of having a solid foundation upon which to build and provides a metaphor representing the structures teachers must put in place if they are to be successful in their teaching endeavors.

In the classroom, the rain will come down. It is inevitable. However, if classrooms are built on a solid foundation, beginning before and continuing after the children walk through the door, the classroom *will* stand firm. As children cross the threshold of the classroom, it is imperative that teachers work aggressively and continuously to establish the conditions necessary for effective teaching and learning.

"What we have learned is that well-managed classrooms exist because teachers have clear ideas of the types of classroom conditions and student behaviors necessary for a healthy learning environment. They not only have clear ideas, they work to create these conditions" (Everston, Emmer, and Worsham 2003, ix). These conditions include the optimal instructional practices provided through the gradual release of responsibility model of instruction and through proactive and ongoing classroom management practices. A well-managed classroom does not just *happen*. It is organized and maintained through the conscious and ongoing efforts of an effective teacher.

General Beliefs About Children

"Good management, like good teaching, is a matter of solving problems and helping people do their best" (Kohn 1993, 16). It is the responsibility of good teachers to do just that.

One component of effective literacy instruction is working with small groups of children. In their efforts to manage small groups successfully, the number one question they often ask is "But, what about the rest of the class?" Inherent to answering that question is an investigation of generalized beliefs about teaching and learning. What teachers actually *do* when engaged in the act of teaching is motivated by what they *believe* about learners and the processes that underlie learning (Cambourne 1988). This leads to two questions that teachers need to ask continually in both their planning and instruction (Platt 1996):

- **Why am I doing this?**
- **How is it good for children?**

To answer the preceding questions, teachers must first recognize some common beliefs about children and learning. Such beliefs often grow out of teachers' own experiences, but the following are some generalized beliefs about children:

- **Children want to be successful learners.**

"A child does not have to be especially motivated or rewarded for learning, in fact, the thrust to learn is so natural that being deprived of the opportunity to learn is aversive. Children will struggle to get out of situations where there is nothing to learn" (Smith 1985, 89).

- **Children are always learning.**

  "Learning is what children do best, and under the right conditions they do so easily" (Sharon Taberski 1996).

- **Children get better at whatever they practice.**

  "Practice makes perfect" is a well-known and universal saying. However, it may not always be for the best "…asking children to take one practice test after another might reinforce ineffective test-taking strategies" (Calkins 1998, 70).

- **Children seek order.** (Note: *Order* is markedly different than *control*.)

  "But to say that children need structure or guidance is very different from saying they have to be controlled" (Kohn 1993, 32–33).

In relation to the beliefs about children, the following beliefs about management and behavior emerge:

- **Children will function within whatever parameters are (or are not) set for them.**

- **If a situation is engineered such that a learner is sure to fail, he or she will work to be successful in other endeavors (e.g., disrupting the classroom, becoming the class clown, etc.).**

- **Children may not necessarily be learning what teachers think they are teaching.**

- **If misbehavior is practiced, students get better at misbehaving.**

It is the set of beliefs teachers hold about teaching and learning that drive the instructional decisions they make. If those decisions are good ones, they lead to the establishment of a solid foundation that is absolutely necessary for optimal learning to occur. In his book *The Process of Education*, Jerome Bruner quotes one of his peers who states explicitly "When you teach well, it always seems as if 78 percent of the students are above the median" (1960). Reflective teachers must consider the alternative to such teaching: Could poor teaching possibly result in 78 percent of student functioning below the median? The primary responsibility of teachers is to coordinate an environment that is most conducive to successful teaching and learning. Just as the wise man built his house upon the rock, the classroom foundation must be thoughtfully structured so that it too will stand firm.

Building a Solid Foundation

Returning to the metaphor presented at the beginning of the introduction, when it comes to effective literacy instruction, it is in every teacher's best interest to follow the steps of the wise man who built his house upon the rock. It is crucial for teachers to take the time to build a solid foundation based on good classroom management before venturing on to more academic pursuits.

An effective classroom is built on many firmly rooted structures and routines. In an effective classroom, the teacher will take a considerable amount of time to address the basic organization of the structures of the classroom, ranging from the organization of materials and space to the use of time to assessment and assessment practices. It is also critical that the teacher spend sufficient time initially and in an ongoing fashion to establish the routines of the classroom. A classroom is a crowded place full of materials, children, teachers, and opportunities to learn. These must be recognized and embraced to build a fully functional foundation.

Reflecting on yourself as a successful learner puts you in a proper frame of reference to explore what effective teaching is all about. "In an ideal world, if you wanted to become competent in something you did not know, you would seek an expert teacher who could give you a great deal of personal attention ...taught this way, you would ...become competent in a reasonable amount of time" (Glasser 1993, 85). Over time, an expert teacher supports learners in acquiring new skills, strategies, understandings, and behaviors through a gradual release of responsibility from teacher to learner (see the Gradual Release of Responsibility Model). Professionals such as Brian Cambourne (1988), Don Holdaway (1979), Ellin Oliver Keene (1997), Fyodor Vygotsky (1962), and Margaret Mooney (1990) address, in their own ways, the gradual release of responsibility theory, which supports a learner as he or she gradually works to take on new learning. Each also recognizes the role of the teacher in determining where each learner is on the developmental learning curve as well as determining the best manner in which to support the continued progress of that learner.

Generally, the gradual release of responsibility theory has been applied to the instruction of reading and writing. The value of this model of teaching and learning also needs to be recognized in relation to developing an effective learning environment. A teacher needs to take into account the fact that students need time and support to take on the responsibility necessary to operate successfully within the classroom.

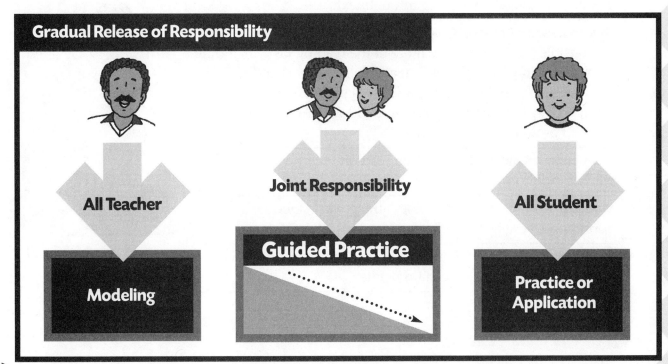

Gradual Release of Responsibility

All Teacher

Joint Responsibility

All Student

Modeling

Guided Practice

Practice or Application

Adapted from Pearson, P. D. and Gallagher, M. C. 1983. The instruction of reading comprehension. *Contemporary Educational Psychology*, 8, 317–344.

Effective Instruction Begins with Classroom Management

It is only after the solid foundation of classroom management has been established that effective literacy instruction can begin. Effective teachers of reading and writing who are familiar with the natural learning model embodied by the gradual release of responsibility theory have grown comfortable in the knowledge that to acquire a new skill or strategy, learners need to be provided with a scaffolded form of instruction wherein the new skill is modeled *for* them, then approached in a shared fashion *with* the help of a more knowledgeable individual, then attempted by the learner in a supportive environment (Mooney 1990). The benefits of adopting the gradual release of responsibility theory should be recognized both within the establishment of a well-managed classroom and as a healthy and universally successful model for literacy teaching and learning.

In solid literacy instruction, teachers embrace the gradual release of responsibility theory and bring it to life within their classrooms through the use of effective instructional strategies that fall into the following categories:

- **Modeled Reading:** The teacher reads aloud, while the children are exposed to the joys and mechanics of reading.

- **Shared Reading:** The teacher reads a text visible to all students (big book, chart, overhead text, class set of multiple copies), as the children follow along and provide input as requested by the teacher.

- **Interactive Reading:** The teacher and student work together, almost equally, to navigate their way through text.

- **Guided Reading (or Small Group Reading Instruction):** The child is responsible for 90 percent or more of the reading task, including comprehension. The teacher is available to support and redirect, minimally. This naturally indicates that children will be grouped by ability and/or need and will work one on one or in small groups with the teacher.

- **Independent Reading:** The children read on their own as the teacher monitors regularly.

- **Modeled Writing:** The teacher does all the work, modeling appropriate strategies for the children to learn from.

- **Shared Writing:** The teacher does most of the work but invites students to participate at certain points.

- **Interactive Writing:** This is similar to shared writing, only the children take on even more responsibility. This is characterized by a "sharing of the pen."

- **Guided Writing:** This parallels guided reading—the children are nearly independent at this level in their writing and the teacher serves as a guide and a coach.

- **Independent Writing:** Children write independently, supported by regular monitoring by the teacher.

Within any classroom, there is a range of learners with varied needs. To meet their needs, teachers must, at times, engage in whole group instruction. After all, there are large numbers of students in most classrooms, and there are a number of skills and strategies that must be introduced. Within whole group instructional models, teachers have the opportunity to explore information that, for some students, will be an introduction, for some will be a review, and for others will be a reinforcement of something they are in the process of coming to understand.

Teachers also have the responsibility for providing instruction at each individual learner's point of need. At times, they may provide this instruction in small group settings and at times on a one-to-one basis. The balance between whole group, small group, and individual instruction also requires a system that allows students to be comfortable and successful in an independent fashion.

It is to this end that this book has been organized, designed, and written. Within an instructional model based on the gradual release of responsibility theory, children need opportunities to work both with and without assistance during a typical classroom day (Dorn 1998). Teachers must seriously consider what to do with the rest of the class while they are working with a single child or a small group of students.

It is also important to remember that table groups and center (or station) groups should not be aligned with reading group assignments. There is nothing more boring that spending an entire school day surrounded by the same four or five children. Mixing up these groups also ensures that teachers will not have all of the struggling readers, behavior problems, and so on together during independent and small group time. Mixing groups at these times is also one of the simplest solutions to management problems.

Armed with the knowledge that the gradual release of responsibility learning theory is truly an effective one and pairing that with the assertion made by Danielson that "the best instructional techniques are worthless in an environment of chaos" (1996, 83) it makes sense for teachers to focus first on classroom management and then on academic instruction if they hope to be optimally successful in their instruction.

Section Overviews
·······································

Section   Chapters 1, 2, and 3 investigate the necessity of organizing for space, time, and assessment. They help you answer the question "How can I make the most of what I have to work with?"

Section   Chapters 4 and 5 provide a detailed look at establishing routines and planning for the first most crucial weeks of the year. It is in this window of time that the groundwork for a year's worth of success or failure is laid.

Section   Chapters 6 and 7 examine dozens of ways in which you can structure independent and small group work time.

The appendix provides a myriad of blackline masters that you may photocopy or adapt to use in your classroom.

Efficiency and Effectiveness Tasks are scattered throughout the text to help you practice and reflect on the strategies in this book.

Section 1

Creating a Climate Conducive to Learning

"Fail to plan? Plan to fail!"

This contemporary proverb sums up the importance of classroom management. When it comes to planning for success in teaching and learning, three key components come to mind:

- **Organizing for space**
- **Organizing for time**
- **Organizing for assessment**

All three of these components are elements teachers must plan for. If teachers allow themselves to be limited, controlled, or overwhelmed by them, their instruction (and general disposition) will surely suffer. It is quite possible to finish nearly every school day feeling calm and refreshed, but this is not something that just happens, it is something that teachers must organize and plan for.

To create an efficient and instructionally effective environment "…you and your students need an orderly environment with minimal disruption and wasted time, leaving everyone free to concentrate on the critical tasks of learning. Carefully planned procedures help create this environment" (Danielson 1996, 20).

Chapter 1

Organizing for Space

My first classroom more closely resembled an airport runway than it did a venue for learning. I would say it was roughly 15 feet wide and 40 feet long—the back half of what used to be the stage of an auditorium. The one existing wall was a gigantic mural featuring Sesame Street characters, each one about 10 feet tall. The two side walls were cinder-block stairwells that, other than functioning as entryways and exits, served no purpose to anyone other than aiding the occasional parent that discovered their usefulness in observing his or her child (and me) without being seen. An unstable, towering stack of boxes containing old basals, recycled paper, and half-used art supplies ran the length of what used to be the stage front, making up the fourth and final wall, which also doubled as the front of my room. I quickly came to the realization that I needed to take control of the space I had, or it would take control of me.

While there are some things about a classroom that teachers cannot control (the location of walls, doors, windows, plugs, and the number of students) there are many elements that teachers can control. The physical set-up of teachers' classrooms is a direct reflection of their beliefs about teaching and learning. "The organization and look of our rooms, the materials we use, and the way we structure the day send a powerful message to children and parents about our attitudes toward teaching and our expectations for our children… Our classrooms should reflect our goals" (Taberski 2000, 33).

Classroom teachers spend a phenomenal amount of time considering every element of their classroom environment, knowing the powerful influence the emotional and physical state of the room has in organizing for optimal teaching and learning. When looking at a classroom, teachers should consider what it feels like, what it looks like, and what it sounds like.

Efficiency and Effectiveness Task

Complete the following checklists to see what your classroom feels, looks, and sounds like (see the appendix for full-page blackline masters). These are questions that you can ask as you do a 360 degree virtual tour of the classroom. Standing in one place, do a complete circle, soaking up everything about the environment. Some teachers find it valuable to sit in a student desk for a different perspective or ask a peer to come in and work through the questions together. The rest of this chapter discusses each of the checklist items in detail.

How Does the Classroom Look?

✔ Is there a teacher's desk? If so, where is it? How and when is it used?

✔ How are student desks or tables organized?

✔ Are there logical pathways for movement?

✔ Is there a floor space large enough for the whole group to sit comfortably?

✔ Is there some place for children to work quietly?

✔ Are materials well organized and accessible?

✔ Is there an overabundance of workbooks and worksheets?

✔ Is there a lot of unnecessary clutter?

✔ Is there a word wall? What is on it? How is it being used? (This should be empty initially, and grow as the year goes on.)

✔ Is there a letter line? What is on it? How is it used?

✔ What else is on the walls?

✔ Is there a classroom library? How is it organized?

✔ Is there a Big Book stand for shared reading?

✔ Are there writing spaces available for modeling?

✔ Do the students have a sense of how the environment has been organized?

How Does the Classroom Feel?

✔ Do I feel comfortable as I enter?

✔ Do I get a peaceful sense of order, or am I overwhelmed by a sense of chaos?

✔ Is this a place where I would enjoy spending six (give or take) hours a day? Would I want to learn here? Could I learn here?

✔ What appears to be important in this room?

How Does the Classroom Sound?

✔ Whose voices do I hear? What are they saying?

✔ How effectively can the teacher get students' attention?

How Does the Classroom Feel?

When considering the "feel" of a classroom, a teacher addresses the degree to which the learning environment is safe, comfortable, and pleasant. "Is this a place where I would want to spend hours a day learning with and from others? Do I feel good being here?" are questions that teachers might ask when evaluating their classroom environment.

Everyone has experienced uncomfortable environments in the past—a restaurant in which you hold concerns about the cleanliness of the kitchen, an electronics store in which you are overwhelmed by the frenzied environment and the pressure of the employees to make a quick decision, or a doctor's office that does not provide a caring atmosphere but rather a rushed feeling of being another faceless individual in a never-ending list of patients. In all of these situations, you, as a customer, develop a "feel" or a "sense" as to what that business is all about. The business within a classroom is not altogether different. Take a closer look at what lies behind the questions posed in the previous checklist in the Efficiency and Effectiveness Task.

Do I Feel Comfortable as I Enter?

Glasser (1993) believes that a classroom environment must be warm and supportive for quality teaching and learning to occur. It is a teacher's responsibility to organize for such an environment. The tone of a classroom envelops teachers and students the second they cross its threshold. Children know almost immediately whether they have entered a forum for learning in which they would feel comfortable making mistakes and celebrating successes. This feeling is almost tangible in some classrooms, and it is imperative that this tone is a positive one. Whether teachers have children of their own, they should ask themselves "Could I joyfully leave my child (or sibling or niece or nephew or grandchild) in this room for a day? Will he or she be loved and nurtured and come home happy and overflowing with new things that he or she learned that day?"

Do I Get a Peaceful Sense of Order, or Am I Overwhelmed by a Sense of Chaos?

It is much easier to learn in a place of order or one that is characterized by structure than a classroom that is ruled by chaos or a lack of attention to organization. It is important to note that there is a distinction between an *orderly* learning environment and one that is *controlled*. A classroom that is well organized and emanates a sense of promise, efficiency, and clear expectations is orderly. A classroom that is artificially controlled leaves children with an uncomfortable feeling, almost fearful of what would happen if they unknowingly violated one of the "rules."

On the other hand, some classrooms can be characterized by their utter lack of order or structure. When you enter such environments, you get the feeling that everything has been haphazardly organized, from the learners to the learning. These rooms may be loud, unruly, and chaotic.

In an effort to establish order in their classrooms, teachers must again remind themselves that there is a distinct difference between children functioning in an ordered environment, responsible for making choices about their behavior, and a teacher asserting *control* over the students, with little attention to students' needs as learners.

Section 2 provides greater detail on how to go about establishing a teaching environment that is free of chaos and disarray, and, instead, characterized by seamless order that comes about as a result of the joint efforts of the teacher and students.

> To devise flexible and reasonable rules for children, preferably by working *with* them to solve problems rather than imposing these rules on them, is very different from control on the one hand and a laissez-faire approach on the other ... Control breeds the need for more control, which then is used to justify the use of control. (Kohn 1993, 33)

I once heard an odd metaphor comparing children to fleas. Fleas, it seems, are very easy to train. You place them in a jar and cover it. The insects very quickly learn the limits of their environment and leap up, stopping just below the place where they had recently come in contact with the lid. Interestingly enough, if the lid is then removed, the fleas continue to leap up to just below where the lid used to be and no higher. They have learned their limits and continue to function within them. The comparison made to children suggests that if we can clearly define the parameters within which they are allowed to function, they will do so. I have no idea whether fleas can be trained in this manner, and I certainly do not think we should liken children to insects; however, I do believe that children do a marvelous job of functioning within the parameters we set for them. The difference between an orderly classroom and a chaotic one may very well be the difference between well defined and logical parameters, and having poorly defined limits, or none at all.

Is This a Place Where I Would Enjoy Spending Six (give or take) Hours a Day? Would I Want to Learn Here? Could I Learn Here?

This item relates to the tone and the feel of the classroom. "Would I *want* to spend time here?" Brain research studies show that emotion drives learning and attention (Caine and Caine 1994). If students are in an unpleasant, unenjoyable, or threatening environment, they will downshift (Hart 1983) to the lowest form of learning—rote memorization. Rote memorization is, in effect, a survival skill: Just tell me what to do and I will do it! Others disagree with the downshifting metaphor. Instead, they believe that students' emotions intensify to put them on high alert when they feel threatened (Sylwester 1998). They react unconsciously and automatically: Act first—think later. Either way, children will not be in a state conducive to learning.

As stated in the introduction, children want and need to learn. When they are not able to do so, they will engage in other, less-desirable, behavior. If a child is faced with tasks that are too challenging, too simple, or that leave unfilled time, he or she will take the opportunity to entertain him- or herself with something that would be more engaging. Many times this takes the form of inappropriate behavior that will disallow that child and possibly other students to learn.

What Appears to Be Important in This Room?

The answer to this question provides insight into what the teacher sees as important. "What teachers actually *do* when engaged in the act of teaching is motivated by what they *believe* about the processes that underlie learning" (Cambourne 1988, 17). The decisions teachers make on a daily basis are directly influenced and guided by what they believe about the processes of teaching and learning (Cambourne 1988). Not only does instruction reflect a teacher's beliefs, the entire classroom environment becomes a product of what that teacher believes.

Reflecting on the answers to the questions about how your classroom feels (refer to the Efficiency and Effectiveness Task) will set you on the road to confirming or reorganizing your current beliefs about teaching and learning in your classroom. Determine where it is that you feel that you might need to spend more time in energy in your instruction, and then focus on that element.

> ## Efficiency and Effectiveness Task
>
> You may want to investigate what appears important in your room by inviting a peer to observe you or by videotaping yourself on several occasions to measure yourself more objectively.
>
> **Have your peer answer or ask yourself the questions below** (see the appendix for full-page blackline masters).
>
> - Where does the teacher position him- or herself for instruction?
> - Is there absolute silence, except for when the teacher is speaking or asking a question?
> - Is there an imposing feeling of control?
> - Does the teacher go to the children or do the children have to go to the teacher?
> - If the children go to the teacher, is there a long line of children constantly seeking help or approval?
> - Is covering the content, regardless of student needs, an overshadowing characteristic?
> - Physically, how are things organized?
> - How does the teacher convey that books and reading are important? Are books easily accessible to students?
> - How does the teacher honor children's work? Is the work visible?
> - Do learners appear to be self-motivated and independent?

How Does the Classroom Look?

In his infinite wisdom, Don Holdaway (1979) maintains that "much teaching energy is spent on compensating for an unfavorable environment. It would be far more sensible to use our energies first on the environment itself" (15). There is no one best way to organize the physical elements of a classroom. Teachers must look individually at their classrooms and the physical elements that they contain as the tools to craft instruction. Teachers must determine what it is that they are hoping to achieve and accomplish and seriously consider how it is that the organization of the physical environment can either help or hinder them as they take on the responsibility for doing so. A carpenter might be able to pound a nail in using a screwdriver but that would obviously not be the most efficient and effective manner in which to achieve that goal. The same is true for the decisions teachers make about how to use their classroom tools. If teachers organize materials and environments wisely in the first place, they will save countless hours and great stress as they proceed through the year.

The following are areas of the classroom, or elements within it, that teachers should address when considering their room arrangement.

Is There a Teacher's Desk? If So, Where Is It? How and When Is It Used?

> Some years ago, Regie Routman convinced me to eliminate the teacher's desk to help convey the idea that the classroom is child-centered. I found it difficult at first. Where would I put my lesson plan book? Where would the student teacher and I pile office memos and handouts? I have compromised by using a small table that is not, as my desk was, the first thing you notice when you enter the classroom.
> (Servis 1999, 16)

You may consider following Routman's advice by getting rid of your monstrous, space-eating desk. The need for space is great enough as it is, why exacerbate the problem by having a piece of furniture that is not even (or rarely) used during the school day? The role of the teacher in any classroom is to be in the immediate presence of one, some, or all of the students. If children are reading, writing, or working independently, the teacher should be working with a small group or conferencing one on one with a student.

Obviously, the teacher's desk is a location to store important items such as office supplies, files, and plan books. However, you may  consider the possibility of organizing an alternate storage system for these items that would not take up so much space. Try using a small table or a student desk. Getting rid of the desk will also help you with another issue—hanging onto unnecessary clutter. Think of all the things that end up on your desk, just because the space is there.

If you decide to keep your desk, it is best to move it to the back of the room. Then its presence does not dominate the classroom, sending the message "This is my classroom. You are here for me." as opposed to "This is our classroom, and I am here for you."

How Are Student Desks or Tables Organized?

Joanne Hindley (1996) quotes her colleague Isabel Beaton at the Manhattan New School, "Geography is everything. I realized that I needed to figure out what I wanted to happen and how my classroom geography could support and enhance—or inhibit and deter—those goals" (5).

Organizing desks in rows is a common way to organize the classroom; however, it is not the most conducive arrangement to learning. Humans are social beings and they need to talk. Talking is part of learning—it is how children solidify the information that they have acquired and best process new information as they integrate that into their existing schema. Because the social environment is closely connected to—in fact, imbedded in—the learning environment, teaching children how to get along with others is certainly an appropriate instructional practice.

The following are possible room arrangements for kindergarten, first grade, and second/third grade.

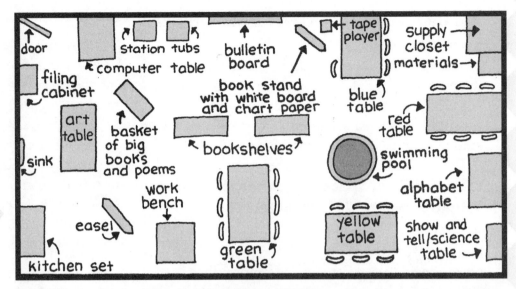

Kindergarten

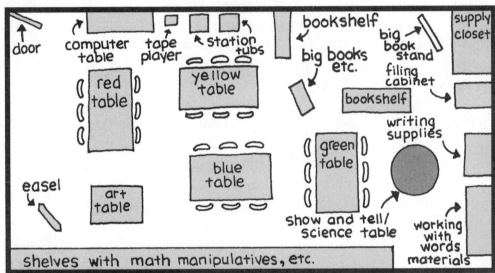

First Grade

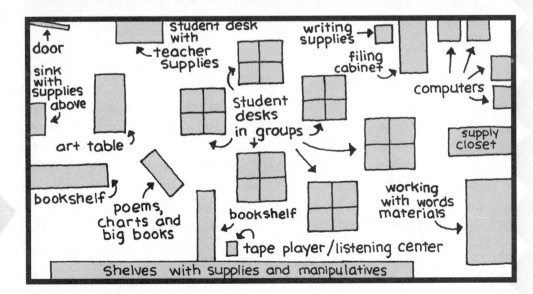

Second/ Third Grade

Classroom Organization and Management: *Strategies for Establishing and Maintaining an Effective Learning Environment*

21

Are There Logical Pathways for Movement?

The best way to answer this question is to take a walking tour of the classroom to ensure there are appropriate pathways for movement. Also make sure that furniture and materials are organized in such a fashion that teachers and students can easily access instructional materials.

Is There a Floor Space Large Enough for the Whole Group to Sit Comfortably?

If teachers are going to engage in effective literacy instructional practices and plan on generating a true classroom community, they need to organize their environment to have adequate space for the group to congregate. "Teachers who rearrange furniture throughout the day frequently become frustrated …it is easier in the long run to designate a section of the room as the gathering place, and then design the rest of the classroom around it" (Taberski 2000, 21).

I unintentionally designed my first classroom with one gigantically long and narrow passage that made my travel path easier but also invited children to barrel straight across the classroom at top speed. A quick turn of a bookshelf required a few additional steps on my part but, at the same time, slowed my students down considerably—a change that was worth the minor inconvenience to me.

In your own classroom, try to seek out a cozy corner for this floor space. You also might want to make sure your back is to the wall so children do not have any option other than to look at you. If you are in front of a window or door or in the inner part of the room, children can easily find all sorts of interesting things to look at instead of focusing their attention on you and the task at hand. Also be sure that there are no distractions in children's immediate presence. If they are sitting right next to baskets of toys or mathematics supplies, they may easily find something more exciting to focus their attention on.

Once you organize your spot, choose a chair for yourself. It is important to be comfortable, but you may want to consider using a student chair as they are lower to the floor and bring you closer to the group. If you are on an adult chair and children are on the floor, there is often a considerable discrepancy between your eye level and theirs. You may appear as if you hold a majestic reign over them as they crane their necks to see. To appreciate the feel of such an instructional setting, consider what it would be like if you were sitting in a workshop or college course and your instructor was standing on a chair teaching. The physical distance between a teacher and learner sends an unspoken message to the learner.

Some classrooms are so small that organizing this floor space becomes an earnest challenge. If you find that you are struggling to organize your classroom to accommodate floor space and have tried rearranging the furniture to no avail, you can teach children how to move minimal furniture quickly to create and instant space. If you do not have a carpeted floor, put sliced tennis balls on the ends of each table and chair leg to reduce noise and increase ease in moving the object; then place an "X" on the floor with tape to indicate where the furniture should be moved to and returned to. Children can rapidly slide back one or two tables and then return them to their original position as needed. It is important to use this as a last resort as every time the furniture has to be moved results in wasted instructional time.

Is There Some Place for Children to Work Quietly?

Students have the right to a working environment that will allow them to be successful. Much of this will be addressed through the guidelines and norms established for the independent work behaviors in the classroom, but it is a good idea to have an area or areas in the classroom specifically designated as peaceful work areas for children who are intensely engaged in learning tasks and do not want to be disrupted. Take care to ensure that such a location does not turn into a hiding spot or a hangout for off task students. There are many locations that can serve dual purposes in a classroom that is short on space. For example, consider using the floor space in the classroom library as a quiet place to spread out and work. Some teachers even allow children to crawl under desks or tables—as long as they are on task and safe.

Are Materials Well Organized and Accessible?

This goes for both student and teacher materials. It is easy to see how well organized a teacher is by taking a quick glance around the room. Are supplies neatly organized and labeled? Or are they piled helter skelter, here and there? What do children's desks look like? Are they overflowing with crumpled paper and books? It is critical for teachers to have a system for themselves and their students.

> **Efficiency and Effectiveness Task**
>
> After reading through all the strategies for organizing the physical classroom, use graph paper to sketch out the boundaries, doorways, locations of plugs, and other unchangeable elements within your classroom. Then use sticky notes cut to size, representing furniture and other movable items, to play with different room arrangements. Make sure to block out floor space for whole group gatherings and other work spaces, trying out as many options as necessary before deciding which one works the best.

My favorite and most productive years as a classroom teacher were the ones when I started the school year with a completely barren classroom. There was nothing on the walls, nothing on the shelves, and nothing on the tables. On the first day of school, we put a basket on each table for snacks and pencil boxes, and every child received one pencil. Later in the day, a single basket of books was introduced but that was it. Nearly every day for the rest of the year, we added items to our room, and it grew slowly over time. When the painting supplies came out of one of the boxes we had lengthy talks about the care and storage of these materials. I rarely found anything out of place these years as the classroom truly belonged to all of us.

Arranging materials is only the first step toward organization. It is also important to teach students how to be respectful of materials. School supplies may very well be the first items children have the privilege of being responsible for. It is the responsibility of teachers to recognize and support them as they learn to care for and respect their materials and those belonging to others, including the teacher. It is a much easier task to accomplish if you ask children to be responsible for a minimum of items initially, and then to broaden that base as they demonstrate readiness.

Is There an Overabundance of Workbooks and Worksheets?

Jeanette Veatch (1997) once stated that if teachers ever have all of their students doing the same thing at the same time, they had better stop and have a think about what they are doing. Having all students working independently on the same type of worksheet is not beneficial in supporting learning. On any given worksheet, there may be ten to twenty items, all focusing on relatively similar tasks. If the child has done the first four or five correctly, you can pretty much assume that he or she understands the task. The rest of the worksheet would then be largely wasted time. On the other hand, if a child gets the first handful of items wrong, he or she has clearly demonstrated that he or she does not understand the task. If he or she is required to complete the worksheet, he or she will undoubtedly continue making the same errors, in effect *practicing* them, getting better and better at doing that task incorrectly. This is a perfect example of how using the two questions from the introduction will help you move to a more reflective practice:

- **Why am I doing this?**
- **How is it good for children?**

Many teachers have also tried to use packets of worksheets as management tools. It is far wiser to invest time and energy into establishing independent work activities that will allow children to engage with tasks that are more meaningful and are directly linked to authentic reading and writing.

Startling as this may sound, the truth is that many children read for a remarkably small percentage of the school day. Researchers have for a long while documented that children in many classrooms spend more time on dittoes and exercises, multiple-choice questions, and language drills than on reading whole texts. Children sometimes spend two-and-a-half hours in reading instruction and only ten minutes of that time actually reading." (Calkins, Montgomery, and Santman 1998, 51)

Efficiency and Effectiveness Task

Collect all the worksheets you used this week. For each one, answer the following questions (you may want to put your answers on sticky notes and attach to each worksheet):

- **Why am I doing this?**
- **How is it good for children?**

What did you learn about your use of worksheets?

If you do choose to use worksheets, be acutely critical of those that you select for use. Ask yourself for every worksheet and every child "Why am I doing this? How is it good for this child?" You may need to take it a step further and ask yourself "How is doing this worksheet going to help this student become a better reader or writer?" If you cannot answer these questions satisfactorily, you need to find alternate activities that will support literacy development. Section 3 provides suggestions for authentic literacy activities your children can engage in instead of staying busy through packets of worksheets or workbook pages.

Is There a Lot of Unnecessary Clutter?

Teachers are notorious for being pack rats. Anything that comes their way seems to find itself a home in the classroom. Even though teachers eventually use some of it, it seems that great quantities of clutter accumulate in each classroom. Some classrooms may even have piles teetering dangerously, somewhat like Sarah Cynthia Sylvia Stout's garbage pile in Shel Silverstein's (1974) poem. There are several problems with this unnecessary accumulation. Some teachers tend to collect so much of it, that when it comes around to being time to use whatever they need, they often struggle to find it because it is buried so deeply in years' worth of collected treasures. You may have found yourself holding onto items for years on end, thinking, "But I might need it someday!" Take a close look at what you have sitting around. The classroom is a home to children for six hours or more every day. Such an overwhelming environment will surely make it harder for students to learn and definitely make it harder for you to teach. A good rule to follow: If you have not used it for a year, get rid of it.

Is There a Word Wall? What Is on It? How Is It Being Used?

If a word wall is being used effectively, it will be 100 percent empty on the first day of school. That is right—100 percent empty. *Teaching Reading and Writing With Word Walls: Easy Lessons and Fresh Ideas For Creating Interactive Word Walls That Build Literacy Skills* (Wagstaff 1999) is full of suggestions for variations on word walls. Wagstaff reminds teachers that a word wall should look different in every classroom and will never look the same from year to year, as it needs to be designed and crafted to meet the unique set of needs being represented in that classroom.

A word wall needs to be located in clear view of the space where modeled and shared writing will occur, and it also needs to be visually accessible to students as they are writing independently. The teacher has a responsibility in modeling how to use this resource on a daily basis. One final concern about word walls relates to the words that make their way onto them: Be hyper-vigilant as to what words appear there, choosing those that will be of greatest benefit to students as they write and spell. Placing every word that children would ever want or need to spell on the wall would be ridiculous. The only result would be ultimate dependency on the wall as a word bank. Certainly some words can be used in this manner, but most of the words appearing on the wall should be there to provide links or connections to other words. If there are important words that students need to be familiar with (science words, mathematical terms, testing vocabulary) you should most certainly post those but not as part of the general word wall. Put up a separate word family for that specific category of words.

The following are some possible ideas for a word wall and word families.

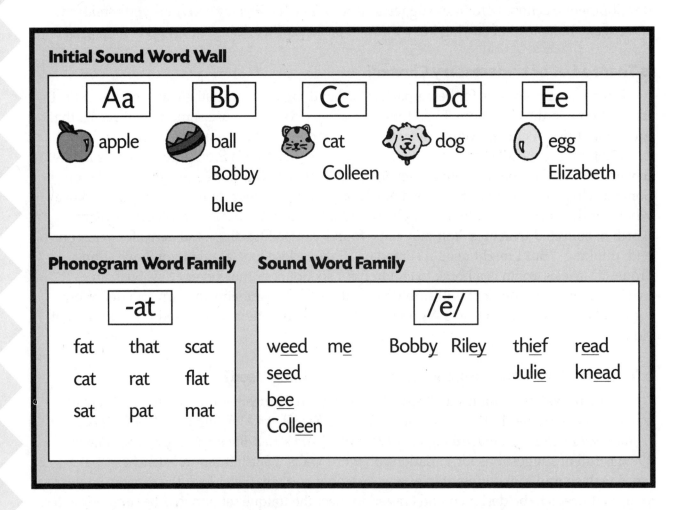

Initial Sound Word Wall

Aa	Bb	Cc	Dd	Ee
apple	ball	cat	dog	egg
	Bobby	Colleen		Elizabeth
	blue			

Phonogram Word Family

-at		
fat	that	scat
cat	rat	flat
sat	pat	mat

Sound Word Family

/ē/

weed   me   Bobby   Riley   thief   read
seed   Julie   knead
bee
Colleen

Is There a Letter Line? What Is on It? How Is It Used?

Nearly every classroom has a letter line prominently displayed above the chalkboard, serving as a model for letter formation for students developing in their penmanship skills. The letter line is for more than merely a reference for letter formation. It is an unparalleled tool for supporting early spellers. In addition to an enlarged letter line, "many teachers use a chart of clear letter forms and simple pictures that provide a clear letter-sound link to key words" (Fountas & Pinnell 1996, 172).

Each letter should be accompanied with a picture that provides an anchor for the sound it represents most often. For example, next to the letter "Bb" would be a ball. Make sure the line is visible to students. This is not necessarily at eye level. A more logical place may be higher up since the eye-level plane is often broken by people, objects, or doorways, leading to more confusion or a complete inability to reference it. Also make sure that the images are obvious to students. Letter lines with uncommon images are better used for vocabulary development. If the goal of the letter line is to assist in the development of phonemic awareness, use a letter line similar to the one shown on this page (see appendix for full blackline master).

What Else Is on the Walls?

Most teachers are familiar with the "Hang in there!" poster with a kitten hanging off a branch. It is cute and has a positive message, but most struggling students do not look up, gather energy from that cat, and think "If he can do it, I can do it." When walls are filled with posters like this one, they merely serve as wallpaper. "It is important that child-made charts be at least as numerous as those made by teachers" (Cambourne 1988, 46).

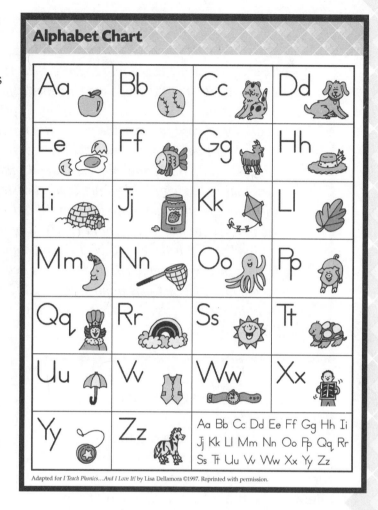

Alphabet Chart

Adapted for *I Teach Phonics...And I Love It!* by Lisa Dellamora ©1997. Reprinted with permission.

Be careful not to fall victim to the "curse of the dot letters." I spent years being heralded for the most glorious bulletin boards and door decorations, but was brought to reality when I finally noticed that all of the artwork that other teachers were so complimentary of made absolutely no impression on my students. As a matter of fact, my students were, for the most part, completely unaware of its existence. I learned fairly quickly—if it is on the walls, it needs to have been created for, with, or by my students.

When working to cover the walls of the classroom, the best resources are the large chart papers filled with modeled, shared, or interactive writing texts you have created jointly with students. They provide meaningful work that will support students as they work to incorporate in their own writing the same strategies you visited as a group.

So what is the best approach when hanging student work? Should teachers edit everything, make it perfect, and then post it? Or, should teachers post less than perfect student work that might advertise incorrect writing elements?

After spending a few days working on a text, I told my students that I was so proud of their efforts that I was going to hang their (unedited) work on the wall outside of the classroom. About half of the kids were thrilled and the other half could care less. I will never forget one student, "But Ms. D., it's wrong! I spelled it all wrong. Don't hang it. It's wrong!" I was working so hard to make the point that I accepted her effort that I completely violated her as a learner. As I posted her work for all to see, she was mad at me and embarrassed—and rightfully so. Up to that point, she was happily taking risks and making mistakes, but when I displayed that to the world, I lost her trust. I certainly could have edited her work to the point of it being perfect and then hung it up, but I did not think that would be fair either. The only message that would have sent would be, "You're not a very good writer, but look at what a great editor I am." I believe that we need to honor children's work, but I am not sure that I have to post their efforts publicly to do that. How would you feel if you were the poorest writer in the room and that fact was publicized weekly? I shudder at the thought of one of my college professors taking one of my essays and stapling it outside his door—no matter how good or bad. Why do it to children?

Irene Fountas and Gay Su Pinnell shared the same wisdom.

The vast majority of work that is published in a classroom can be jointly constructed text that comes from shared or interactive writing lessons. Some of it can come from modeled writing that you do, and a portion should be children's independent writing.

> Since much of the print on display surfaces will serve as reading material, the print should be in standard spelling. Children will use approximated spellings as they construct words in their journals and independent writing, and these may be labeled to honor children's work. Teachers can label these as 'works in progress' to distinguish them from published work." (Fountas and Pinnell 1996, 46)

Similar to Fountas and Pinnell's suggestion of noting "works in progress," you might create an entire bulletin board dedicated to housing all of the odds and ends of writing samples that students want to post. Keep a stack of 4x6 inch cards that say, "_____ made this!" and every time a child wants to add something to the board, you can add his or her name to the card and post it. Students will be thrilled to be published, and you can take comfort knowing that this is self-selected participation. It is important to note that this bulletin board serves as a celebration not as a writing resource. In the second and third grade, you might post large resealable bags with each child's name. The child is allowed to choose whatever he or she would like to put into the resealable as a celebration of his or her work.

Efficiency and Effectiveness Task

What is on your walls? Fill out the chart at the right (see the appendix for a full blackline master). As you go through your day, circle the items your students use or attend to regularly. Star the items you model the use of. After about a week, review your list and decide which materials on your walls are valuable instructional materials and which need to go.

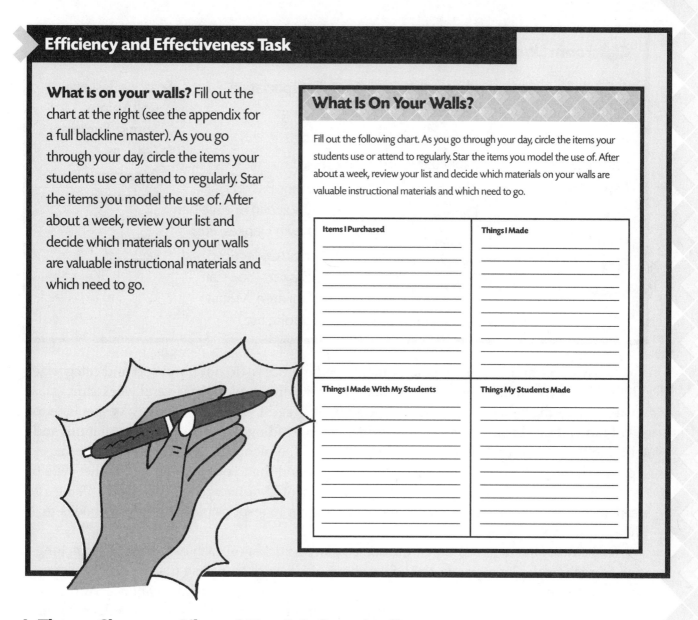

What Is On Your Walls?

Fill out the following chart. As you go through your day, circle the items your students use or attend to regularly. Star the items you model the use of. After about a week, review your list and decide which materials on your walls are valuable instructional materials and which need to go.

Items I Purchased	Things I Made

Things I Made With My Students	Things My Students Made

Is There a Classroom Library? How Is It Organized?

The best way to organize the classroom library is the way that is going to benefit you directly; however, you may find that in looking to the experts (such as the Barnes and Noble and Borders bookstores), you can learn a lot. Their texts are largely organized by category and sometimes by level of difficulty, such as the Children's and Young Adult's sections, but for the most part, the reader is responsible for deciding which book is most appropriate for him or her. Whichever system you choose, make sure to review the system with students so they can put the books away correctly.

If you choose to organize your classroom library into categories, you might start with Caldecott winners, animals, insects, or fairy tales. The following is a suggested list of categories.

Classroom Library Suggested Categories:

Animals	Plants	Transportation	Seasons Baskets
Caldecott Winners	Poetry	Feelings	(Fall, Winter,
Newbury Winners	Colors	Sports	Spring, Summer)
Fairy Tales	Alphabet	Food	Holiday Baskets
Mysteries	Numbers	Author Baskets	(Valentine's Day,
School	Dinosaurs	(Norman Bridwell,	Halloween,
Friendship	Weather	Kevin Henkes, etc.)	Christmas,
Pets	Insects	Series/Collection	Hanukkah,
Ocean	Old Favorites	Baskets (Box Car	Kwanza)
		Children, M&M	
		books, etc.)	

To save time and to include your students in the process, do not try to sort and categorize all the books yourself. If you have hundreds of books, this could take several weekends. Instead, elicit the help of your students. You might suggest "Hey kids, I have a basket here for all of our Clifford books. If you see one while you're reading this week, please pull it out and put it in the basket marked 'Norman Bridwell.' He's the man that wrote them all." For the next week or so, your students will do all the work, and then you can look for another type of text. This method may take longer, but the benefits would outweigh the time factor. Being responsible for the sorting results in students being more responsible for returning books to their appropriate basket in the long run.

To maintain the organization of the books, place a sticker on each basket with a matching one on each book. For example, the books about plants may all have a tree sticker. Take care to introduce the books in your library slowly and over time rather than all at once. Add only a small selection of books each week, gradually building up the library to aid students rather than overwhelm them.

Is There a Big Book Stand for Shared Reading?

Effective teachers engaging in whole-group, shared-reading instruction and mini-lessons use some sort of stand on a daily basis. It is extremely challenging to balance a big book on your lap at the same time you are trying to make a teaching point. This stand needs to have a prominent place in the classroom and be in good condition. If funds are not available to purchase a stand, check out the local discount stores for an inexpensive child's easel that can be used as a stand by simply placing a board across the paint tray to create a flat surface. Or, try to connect with a local high school or vocational school with a woodshop class that can custom design a stand.

Are There Writing Spaces Available for Modeling?

The best surfaces for modeled and shared writing are either overhead projectors or sturdy easels with either white boards or paper to write on. Traditional wall-mounted chalkboards or blackboards do not provide an optimal instructional situation. Shared- and modeled-writing activities are intimate teaching and learning opportunities that require consistent eye contact with learners. If you are writing on a wall-mounted board, every time you write, you have to turn completely and put your back to the students' faces. This makes it impossible for you to recognize nods of understanding or points of confusion that will require further attention in your instruction—you cannot read the eyes and faces of students if your back is to them. If you write on a slanted surface that you sit *next* to, you can maintain eye contact for a majority of the instructional time, and then just shift your gaze to the paper when necessary.

One of the best writing surfaces, of course, is the overhead projector. It allows you to write in a normal fashion, more true to size, and maintain near constant eye contact with your audience. One of the most successful uses of the overhead projector is when it is flat on the floor rather than on a table or a stand. When it is on the floor, you can sit and look right into the eyes of all of your students as they cluster around you. Some teachers find that they are more comfortable placing the overhead projector on a child's desk, minus the leg extensions, and sitting next to it on a child's chair—closer to the floor than if the projector were on a four foot cart but not all the way down on the floor.

Do Students Have a Sense of How the Environment Has Been Organized?

Children should be able to take guests through their classroom on a tour, identifying different areas and materials and their purposes. Joanne Hindley shares a personal discovery related to such a task.

If students are unable to articulate the reasons for the objects and structures that are in the classroom setting, teachers must consider their value. If children are blind to their environment and do not understand what the word wall is for or how the classroom library is organized, it is probably time to take a step back and review or introduce those areas. It may end up that there are some elements that can be removed, clearing up more time or space for valuable instructional activities.

I realized this was something I needed to think more about when a group of teachers visited my own classroom. I asked a few students to take them on a "walking tour" of our room and point out anything they felt the visitors should know about. Later, in discussing the morning visit, the teachers commented on how well the students seemed to know their space. But as they listed the different areas of the room the children had pointed out, I was more struck by what the children left out than by what they included. They never mentioned numerous bulletin boards, and the teachers noted that they skimmed right over whole sections of the room. These, I realized, were the areas the children never interacted with. (Hindley 1996, 6)

Efficiency and Effectiveness Task

Invite your students to give a tour of your classroom to one of your colleagues. After the tour, sit down and discuss what the students pointed out and what they left out. Return to the room arrangement task you completed earlier in this chapter. What physical parts of the room need to be changed? What is on the walls that needs to be addressed with students or redone? Note on your room arrangement chart which changes you would like to make immediately and which you will implement the following school year.

How Does the Classroom Sound?

Organizing for space in the classroom is more than simply what goes in it. You also need to take a closer look at what goes on in it. As the old saying goes: It is not what you have, it is how you use it.

Within a well-managed classroom, there will be noise. Caine and Caine (1994) include in their twelve principles of brain-based learning that the human brain is a social brain and that people need to talk as they learn and process new information. Learners solidify concepts as they reflect on them orally and work to understand new learning together. Teachers must honor this by not only giving students permission and time to talk but by teaching them how to do so in a productive manner. Productive talk is not yelling and hollering; nor is it talking in a respectable tone on a subject completely unrelated to the task at hand.

Teachers often report that when they begin using groups, they are bothered by the increased noise level. A common guideline is the use of the "six-inch" or "twelve-inch" voice. Another is to speak quietly enough so that students in nearby groups can't hear or aren't distracted. "Whisper voices" does not work well as a guideline, because groups usually can't work efficiently and conduct conversations while whispering. (Everston, Emmer, and Worsham 2003, 116)

Whose Voices Do I Hear? What Are They Saying?

If a classroom resonates constantly with the teacher's voice, something is wrong. A necessary component of learning is talking. When children talk over newly acquired information, their brains are able to weigh that information against existing knowledge and file it away in an appropriate and logical location for later retrieval (Caine & Caine 1994). However, there is such a thing as too much student talk. Classrooms can be somewhat noisy places, but they should not be consistently characterized as such. The nature of the noise is what is important. What are the students talking about? Are students and teachers talking to each other or at each other? Are the volume and tone respectful?

How Effectively Can the Teacher Get Students' Attention?

In a busy classroom, a teacher needs to be able to get the attention of all the students in the classroom. This should happen quickly and without the teacher having to raise his or her voice inappropriately. Refer to Chapter 2 for more information on effective strategies for getting students' attention quickly.

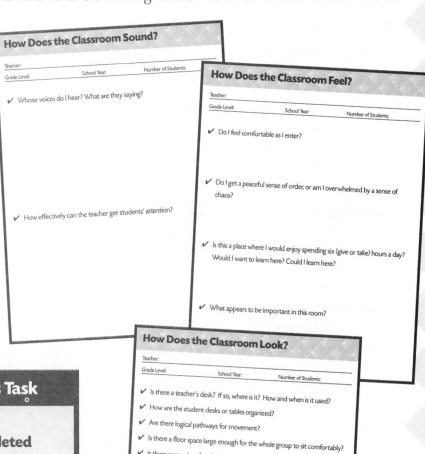

How Does the Classroom Sound?

Teacher:
Grade Level: School Year: Number of Students:

✔ Whose voices do I hear? What are they saying?

✔ How effectively can the teacher get students' attention?

How Does the Classroom Feel?

Teacher:
Grade Level: School Year: Number of Students:

✔ Do I feel comfortable as I enter?

✔ Do I get a peaceful sense of order, or am I overwhelmed by a sense of chaos?

✔ Is this a place where I would enjoy spending six (give or take) hours a day? Would I want to learn here? Could I learn here?

✔ What appears to be important in this room?

How Does the Classroom Look?

Teacher:
Grade Level: School Year: Number of Students:

✔ Is there a teacher's desk? If so, where is it? How and when is it used?
✔ How are the student desks or tables organized?
✔ Are there logical pathways for movement?
✔ Is there a floor space large enough for the whole group to sit comfortably?
✔ Is there some place for children to work quietly?
✔ Are materials well organized and accessible?
✔ Is there an overabundance of workbooks and worksheets?
✔ Is there a lot of unnecessary clutter?
✔ Is there a word wall? What is on it? How is it being used? (This should be empty initially, and grow as the year goes on.)
✔ Is there a letter line? What is on it? How is it used?
✔ What else is on the walls?
✔ Is there a classroom library? How is it organized?
✔ Is there a big-book stand for shared reading?
✔ Are there writing spaces available for modeling?
✔ Do students have a sense of how the environment has been organized?

> ### Efficiency and Effectiveness Task
>
> **Revisit the checklists you completed earlier in this chapter** on How Does the Classroom Feel? How Does the Classroom Look? And How Does the Classroom Sound. Make notes next to the items that you would like to change, modify, or implement after reading through this chapter.

Chapter 2

Organizing for Time

Literacy teachers sometimes overwhelm themselves with their responsibility to cover a large amount of material in a limited amount of time. It is at this point that teachers need to stop and take time to reflect. Refer to the two questions introduced in the Introduction:

• **Why am I doing this?**

• **How is it good for children?**

When teachers focus on the previous questions, they may find that much of the pressure they are feeling has been self-imposed and unnecessary.

Finding Time to Fit It all In

As teachers implement effective teaching practices, their major concern is often the time factor. Many have been heard citing the following, "How on earth can we do all of this? We have so many content area responsibilities, there is no way we can cover all of our curriculum and do all of this literacy stuff!"

Get to know your students, your curriculum, and your materials. Add to that a solid theory to base your instruction on, and time will find you. Always ask: Why am I doing this? How is it good for children?

As I worked with a group of second grade teachers who were struggling to find time to implement the new literacy practices their district was mandating, they gave me an example of a dinosaur unit they needed to teach for science. They explained in great detail all of the things that they incorporated into this extensive study that left them no time to engage in literacy instruction. Equally overwhelmed by the daunting task they were burdened with, I had to agree with them. How on earth would there be time for literacy instruction with all of these content area requirements? In an effort to help them resolve this problem, I asked for the second grade curriculum guide. I found the section that referred to dinosaurs: Children will know and understand that dinosaurs are extinct. *One sentence. That was it! I imagine the unit they created is loads of fun, and I am sure the children learn a great deal about dinosaurs—but at what cost?*

I had only been teaching for four years when I was first stricken with what I call the "filing cabinet flu." It was toward the end of September and time to dig into my files in search of the folders dedicated to Halloween. As I dug through the folders, examples of Halloween artwork, worksheets, writing frames, projects, poems, and all other manner of things began to pile up on the tables, chairs, and floor space surrounding my cabinet. Every file I pulled out provided yet another Halloween-related activity from my undergraduate idea portfolio, my teaching days in numerous classrooms and grade levels, district sharing sessions, countless workshops, and teacher magazines full of cut-and-color activities and art projects. At last the pile stopped growing and I was able to begin my planning. I imagine you can relate to the dismay I experienced when I finally managed to sort through all of the activities and found that to fit them all in, I should have begun my Halloween unit two weeks earlier. Fortunately, I stopped and asked myself: Why am I doing this? How is it good for children? As I considered these two questions, I narrowed down my selections to include only those activities that served a true purpose (not just a "fun" activity), and I reduced my six-week investigation of Halloween to one week. It was a good thing I did as most of my answers to the first question were "Because it matches my theme," "Because it is cute," or "Because the students (or their parents) will like it." I found few answers to the second question.

Ultimately, you need to find and keep activities that are of the most value in developing students academic, social-emotional, and small-motor skills. "In thinking about my beliefs I realize that not every curriculum area can receive equal attention. The only thing we accomplish by spreading ourselves too thin is to set ourselves up to feel mediocre, and teaching deserves much more than mediocrity" (Hindley 1996, xix). It is a good idea to plan most of your instruction *before* you open your filing cabinet. This way, you reflect on your curriculum and the needs of your students first and the contents of the filing cabinet second. If an activity is truly worthwhile, you will remember it when the next year rolls around; however, always check the files, just in case you have forgotten something that would provide a brilliant teaching opportunity.

Scheduling: Putting the Puzzle Pieces Together

Think about organizing your daily schedule as a puzzle that can be put together in a variety of ways. Start out with a list of all the pieces you know you need to include, consider the structures that you cannot control, such as specials, and then start to put together the puzzle.

Even though teachers are first and foremost teachers of literacy, there are many other elements that need to be considered. This section lays out a framework that recognizes the necessary components of a school day. As you are the only one who knows the specifics of your school day, the building of your puzzle is up to you.

The following is a list of daily puzzle pieces for teachers to keep in mind as they structure their day. These vary depending on the grade level, time of year, and the attention span of students. Some days, you might spend a bit more time in one area and a bit less in another:

- **Modeled reading/read-aloud**
- **Shared reading**
- **Small group reading instruction**
- **Independent reading**
- **Whole group writing lesson (modeled, shared, interactive, or mini-lesson)**
- **Guided writing (Small group or one-on-one conferencing)**
- **Independent writing**
- **Independent work**
- **Phonics/Phonemic Awareness/Spelling**
- **Handwriting**
- **Mathematics**
- **Social Studies**
- **Science**
- **Specials**
- **Lunch**
- **Recess**
- **Opening activities**
- **Closing activities**

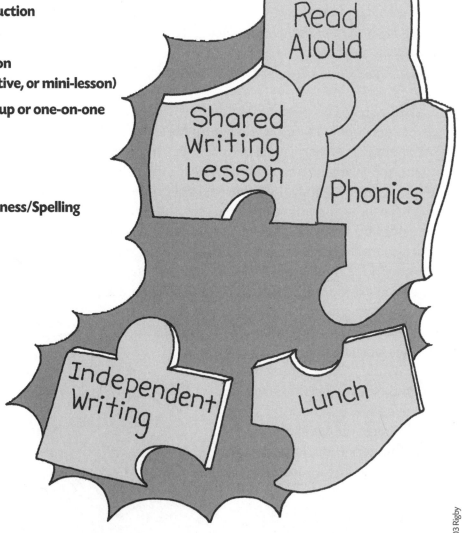

The following chart outlines some suggested time frames, presented by grade level:

	Half Day Kindergarten	Full Day Kindergarten	First Grade	Second Grade	Third Grade
Modeled Reading/Read-Aloud (This time frame does not include any follow-up activities)	5–10 minutes per book	5–10 minutes per book	5–10 minutes	10 minutes	10 minutes
Shared Reading (Break up total timeframes into multiple, shorter lessons.)	15 minutes total	25–30 minutes total	30–40 minutes total	30–40 minutes total	30 minutes total
Guided Reading/Small Group Reading Instruction	5–15 minutes per lesson	5–15 minutes per lesson, 3 groups a day	15 minutes per lesson, 3 groups a day	15–20 minutes per lesson, 3 groups a day	15–20 minutes per lesson, 3 groups a day
Independent Reading	5–10 minutes per day	10–15 minutes per day	10–20 minutes per day, total	15–20 minutes per day, total	15–20 minutes per day, total
Whole Group Writing (This may be modeled, shared, or interactive writing, or take the form of a mini-lesson.)	5–10 minutes per day	10–20 minutes per day, in separate blocks of time	10–20 minutes per day	15–20 minutes per day	20–30 minutes per day, in reasonable blocks of time
Guided Writing	2–8 minutes per child/group	5–10 minutes per child/group	5–10 minutes per child/group	5–10 minutes per child/group	5–10 minutes per child/group
Independent Writing	5–10 minutes per day	5–10 minutes per day	10–20 minutes per day, total	20–30 minutes per day, total	30–45 minutes per day, total
Independent Work	30–45 minutes per day	30–60 minutes per day	45–60 minutes per day	45–60 minutes per day	45–60 minutes per day
Phonics/Phonemic Awareness/Spelling	5–10 minutes explicit, contextualized instruction	5–10 minutes explicit, contextualized instruction	10–15 minutes explicit, contextualized instruction	10–15 minutes explicit, contextualized instruction	10–15 minutes explicit, contextualized instruction
Handwriting (as necessary)	5 minutes per day	5 minutes per day	5 minutes per day	5 minutes per day	5 minutes per day
Mathematics	15–20 minutes per day	15–20 minutes per day	45–60 minutes per day	45–60 minutes per day	45–60 minutes per day
Social Studies	10 minutes per day, alternated with science instruction	15 minutes per day, alternated with science instruction	15–20 minutes per day, alternated with science instruction	20–30 minutes per day, alternated with science instruction	30–45 minutes per day, alternated with science instruction
Science	10 minutes per day, alternated with social studies instruction	15 minutes per day, alternated with social studies instruction	15–20 minutes per day, alternated with social studies instruction	20–30 minutes per day, alternated with social studies instruction	30–45 minutes per day, alternated with social studies instruction
Specials	0–30 minutes for 0–1 per day	0–60 minutes for 0–2 per day	0–60 minutes for 0–2 per day	0–60 minutes for 0–2 per day	0–60 minutes for 0–2 per day
Lunch	NA	20–30 minutes	20–30 minutes	20–30 minutes	20–30 minutes
Recess	15–20 minutes	20–40 minutes total	20–40 minutes total	20–40 minutes total	20–40 minutes total
Opening Activities	15–30 minutes	15–30 minutes	15–30 minutes	10–15 minutes	10–15 minutes
Closing Activities	5–10 minutes	5–10 minutes	5–10 minutes	5–10 minutes	5–10 minutes
TOTAL TIME IN MINUTES:	MINIMUM = 135 minutes/ 2 hours, 15 minutes MAXIMUM: 235 minutes/ 3 hours, 55 minutes	MINIMUM = 185 minutes/ 3 hours, 5 minutes MAXIMUM: 365 minutes/ 6 hours, 5 minutes	MINIMUM = 260 minutes/ 4 hours, 20 minutes MAXIMUM: 455 minutes/ 7 hours, 35 minutes	MINIMUM = 290 minutes/ 4 hours, 50 minutes MAXIMUM: 465 minutes/ 7 hours, 45 minutes	MINIMUM = 335 minutes/ 5 hours, 35 minutes MAXIMUM: 510 minutes/ 8 hours, 30 minutes

The average half-day kindergarten program runs from 9–11:30 and 1–3:30, give or take. The average school day runs from 9–3:30, again, give or take. That provides approximately 150 minutes or 2 1/2 hours per day with half-day programs and 390 minutes or 6 1/2 hours with full-day instructional programs, kindergarten through third grade.

To fit everything in teachers need to create an orderly environment with minimal disruption and wasted time, allowing students to concentrate on their learning (Everston, Emmer, Worsham 2003, 20). To achieve this orderly environment, plan procedures carefully and look closely at the decisions you make as you build your day, returning again to the two questions that guide classroom decisions: Why am I doing this? How is it good for children?

There are many ways that teachers can work to recover lost or hidden time in their daily schedule. Take a close look at the maximum time frames suggested in the chart. Do you have double specials *every* day? Do you spend the maximum amount of time noted on *every* activity *every* day? Could you creatively combine some things, such as incorporating independent reading time into your independent work time? Additional daily independent reading could even occur during the transition into your daily closing. As children wrap up their work, they could sit on the floor with the book they are taking home that day and read.

Another way to find additional instructional time is to write daily "to do" lists for your classroom. Look for the simple tasks that you can get out of the way quickly and easily, or dole out some of those responsibilities to others. Taking attendance or collecting field trip forms does not have to be a lengthy process. You can have children leave money and forms in a basket to check later. Taking attendance can be as simple as taking a look around and identifying empty seats or having children move a card with their name or picture on it from one side of a board to the other, indicating their presence. Fitting it all in is a distinct possibility, as long as you are conscious about how you spend every minute of your day.

Efficiency and Effectiveness Task

Consider working as a private detective within your own classroom and search for those lost instructional minutes and seconds within your day. To begin, fill out the following To Do Lists for an upcoming week (see the appendix for full blackline masters). As you read through the strategies in this section, note where you can make changes or rearrange your priorities to reclaim instructional time.

PM To Do List

Monday	Tuesday	Wednesday	Thursday	Friday
DATE	DATE	DATE	DATE	DATE
11:45	11:45	11:45	11:45	11:45
12:00	12:00	12:00	12:00	12:00
12:15	12:15	12:15	12:15	12:15
12:30	12:30	12:30	12:30	12:45
12:45	12:45	12:45	12:45	1:00
1:00	1:00	1:00	1:00	
1:15	1:15	1:15	1:15	1:15

AM To Do List

Monday	Tuesday	Wednesday	Thursday	Friday
DATE	DATE	DATE	DATE	DATE
8:30	8:30	8:30	8:30	8:30
8:45	8:45	8:45	8:45	8:45
9:00	9:00	9:00	9:00	9:00
9:15	9:15	9:15	9:15	9:15
9:30	9:30	9:30	9:30	9:30
9:45	9:45	9:45	9:45	9:45
10:00	10:00	10:00	10:00	10:00
10:15	10:15	10:15	10:15	10:15
10:30	10:30	10:30	10:30	10:30
10:45	10:45	10:45	10:45	10:45
11:00	11:00	11:00	11:00	11:00
11:15	11:15	11:15	11:15	11:15
11:30	11:30	11:30	11:30	11:45
11:45	11:45	11:45	12:00	
12:00	12:00	12:00	12:00	12:00

Creating More Minutes in the Day

"A study of 105 primary students by Leinhardt, Zigmond, and Cooley (1981) notes that well over an hour each day was spent in waiting, transitions, management, and other activities…" (Allington 2001, 31). Just think of what you could do if you corralled all those wasted minutes and seconds—in total, you would add almost twenty-eight days to the school year.

The following are some suggestions for recapturing this lost time to create more minutes in your day.

Transitions

Children like and thrive on predictable sequences of events in their day (Forester and Reinhard 1994); therefore, it is important to ensure that there are clear routines, including transitions, for students to follow. It is wise to devise a quick attention-getting device. Many teachers ring a bell, some dim the lights, and some raise their hand and wait for others to follow.

> *I have instituted the "Clap-clap, Clap-clap-clap" (two slow claps, three quick claps) as a signal for my students to freeze and repeat the clap. Requiring that they clap back ensures that they drop everything and focus on me, which enables me to deliver concise directions.*

Other suggestions from Everston, Emmer, and Worsham (2003) include:

1. The teacher claps and says, "One, two, three." Students respond, "Eyes on me," and look at the teacher.

   or

   The teacher says, "Thumbs up if you can hear me, Fold your hands if you can hear me, or Clap if you can hear me."

   Each of these signals requires students to engage in a behavior, thus effectively stopping the prior activity.

2. The teacher flips the overhead projector light (or the room lights) on and off twice, then begins clapping and counting, "Ten, nine, eight, seven, six, …one, zip." Students pick up the count as they complete the prior activity, clap and repeat "zip" in unison with the teacher, "zipping" their lips at the end.

3. Ringing a bell or simply saying "Stop, look, and listen" are good signals to use when students are not as interactively engaged.

Whatever system you choose, take the following precautions:

- **If you use the clap system, do not attempt to use it to double as a mathematics activity by changing the pattern every time you do it.** This will not command immediate attention. (Think how ridiculous it would be if the principal changed the fire alarm every time there was a fire or a drill.)

- **Be sure to teach children from day one to freeze and attend to you and only you immediately on recognizing the signal.** If you are not insistent on this from the start, children will not learn to respond appropriately.

- **Be prepared to give immediate, precise, and concise directions within seconds after getting attention.** If you are talking to only one or a few children or dawdle or drone, your students will learn very quickly that your message is unimportant and will continue the activity they were engaged in instead of listening to you.

Bathroom Routines

Do you bring your entire class to the restroom at the same time? How many times a day? How long does it take? Now, you do the math. How much time are you losing? Consider teaching children how to be responsible for going to the bathroom on their own. This would include instruction on the most direct route and how to behave in the hallway, use the restroom, wash hands, leave the bathroom ready for the next person, and return to class promptly. If it is *impossible* for you to organize an independent bathroom procedure, find a way to make use of this time so that it is not lost. Bring along a read-aloud, play phonemic awareness games, or make it part of recess.

"I'm waiting . . . I'm waiting . . . "

If you find yourself standing arms crossed, tapping your foot, repeating this like a broken record or even docking recess time as a trade-off, ask yourself why it is that your students are making you wait. What is it that you are doing next that they are uninterested in? Have you given them the message that promptness is not important and that you will wait for them? If you call students to the floor and then spend five minutes getting ready while they sit there, they will learn quickly that their time is much better spent if they ignore you at first, and then show up five minutes later when you are actually ready.

Students will transition promptly when teachers are fully prepared to move through the lessons of the day. Try not to ask your students to move unless you are ready to proceed with your next lesson. If your classroom is organized and free of clutter, the materials you need will be readily available. If you have worked to streamline your day, you will find that your students will respond appropriately to your call for attention or movement. They will learn quickly that the activities that fill their days are all authentic and engaging activities that serve a purpose. It is very difficult to maintain the attention of students if you lose the momentum and smoothness in the day. Effective teachers are well prepared and maintain an appropriate pace and focus in their lessons. Moving too slowly or quickly, going on tangents, and giving in to distractions will only lead to less productive teaching and learning.

Lining Up

Does it take forever before you can leave your classroom? Try including "lining up" in your instruction. One way to do this is to play mathematical or literacy games. You can say to students, "Line up if . . .

- **you are a three (one, two, four, etc) clapper."** (A three clapper is someone whose name has three syllables—he or she claps once as he or she says each syllable.)
- **you have on /r/ /e/ /d/ (red)."** (Divide words by phonemes, saying each sound.)
- **you have a /d/ /-og/ at home."** (Divide words by onset and rime.)
- **you have the /sh/ sound in your name."** (Indicate sounds for students to listen for in words.)

Another strategy is to switch tasks around in your schedule. For example, end your lesson a minute or two early, and take that time to play phonemic awareness games or sing a song. While the class is engaged in this activity, they can also be putting away textbooks, folders, papers, or whatever it is that often takes five or more extra minutes to take care of before they get into line.

Remember that waiting in line is not an exciting activity that encourages promptness—unless students are vying for a place at the front of the line, which may result in an even larger problem. What can you do to encourage promptness and minimize wasted time? You might consider using standing-in-line time to play daily games with your word wall. For example, "I spy a word with the (long *e* sound)."

Recess

Children need to play, but take care with how much time is being devoted to this activity. Also, think about when you schedule this time.

Do you teach a full day and have trouble getting your students back in from the playground? You might want to try flip-flopping lunch and recess. It might be preferable for students to miss a few minutes of lunchtime than mathematics time.

When I was teaching half-day kindergarten, I had to balance the necessity of play and the amount of transitional time it took us to get dressed and undressed before and after going outside. My solution? I moved recess from the middle of my day to the end. My children got ready to go home and dressed twice as quickly as they were motivated to play (as opposed to standing in line, bored or misbehaving while waiting for their bus) and I rescued valuable instructional time on both sides of a mid-day recess.

If switching around your schedule is not an option, you may want to consider organizing your schedule so that you have students engaged in an enticing activity after lunch or recess. You can reduce transition time dramatically if students start working on independent mathematics or literacy activities immediately after lunch or recess (as opposed to waiting for them, and then launching into a whole group lesson once they are all ready).

Jobs

The lyrics of the classic Beatles' (1967) tune, "I Get by with a Little Help from my Friends," can help here. It is much easier to accomplish nearly anything with a little extra help and that is one of the purposes of classroom jobs. If the classroom truly belongs to the entire community it holds, then all of its members should take an active part in maintaining the dynamic and successful functioning of the system. Holding a classroom job also assists children in developing responsible behavior.

To boost student self-esteem (and make tracking jobs easier for you), consider designating one child as the "Leader for the Day." Students can take turns doing anything and everything that needs to be done that day.

> *I* will never forget this routine during my first year as a teacher. On the first day of school, I had eighteen children, so I organized eighteen jobs thinking I needed to do so to help them all feel good about themselves. Over the next two weeks, my class size grew to twenty-four. As each child came, I created another job. Soon, I not only had so many jobs that I could not remember who was in charge of what, but I also wasted countless minutes daily, arguing about jobs or seeking out the responsible child. In end, by giving everyone *a job, no one felt special or important.*

Snack

Do you have your students sit and wait while you pour drinks and hand out snacks? You may want to consider designating a time for snack and asking your students to bring their own. Snack time is important as students need to fuel their systems on a regular basis, and it also provides an opportunity for them to develop their social and interactive skills as they chat away while they eat.

There are ways to honor both of these needs while not sacrificing valuable instructional and learning time. During snack time, allow students to continue working on whatever independent or small group task they are engaged in while they munch on their snack. Help your students learn that there is no snack "time"; instead, the time they eat their snack runs concurrently with other activities. A child can be snuggled up in the book corner reading while munching away, as another child works in the writing center, pausing every now and then for a nibble. Other children may be working jointly on a task, working, eating, and conversing at the same time.

It is important to teach appropriate routines, and it is well worth the time spent in the long run. For example, make sure children are aware of how sticky fingers can dirty or damage books or computers. This provides an excellent opportunity for a class discussion—children can identify the problem and test out possible solutions. It is also in your best interest to teach your students how to clean up after themselves. They need to be aware of crumbs on the floor and spills on tables and act responsibly by taking care of their mess using paper towels or sponges that are always available to them. If you are worried that some children will forget their snack, organize an "Extra Snack" basket that children can donate to. If they bring a snack they do not like, they can trade. If someone forgets, they can grab one and then bring an extra the next day.

The following are some additional helpful hints for snack time:

- **You might discourage bringing in drinks.** Human bodies are made up of over 80 percent water and the source that comes straight out of the drinking fountain serves as one of the best "brain foods" around. Children should have constant access to water, whether it is through unlimited access to the drinking fountain or a water bottle kept on their desks. If you observe children abusing drinking fountain privileges, do not take them away, ask yourself, "Why? Are they really that thirsty or are they avoiding some other task?" Direct your energy to the source of the problem not toward the symptom.

- **Use this time to encourage good eating habits that will last a lifetime.** Teach your children to bring in foods that are as healthy as possible. Foods without labels (e.g., fruits and vegetables) are the best, but take some time looking at those that do have labels. If you and your students cannot pronounce the words, you might want to help them reconsider using it as fuel for their bodies.

Having a Back-Up Plan

It is important to always have a backup plan that children can easily and automatically refer to, either when they have completed a task early or when you are pulled away from instruction momentarily. The easiest thing to do is to teach your students to have something to read and something to write on immediately available to them. Personal or group book boxes on each table are a must. Include a variety of texts that are both interesting and accessible in these boxes. Add small versions of big books, texts that children have used in small reading groups, child-written and published texts, and copies of old favorites.

> Periodically, you will have to fill in time between activities or before and after major transitions ... Filling these times with a constructive activity is better than trying to stretch out an already completed task or just letting students amuse themselves ... accumulate a file so you will be ready with a filler when one is needed (Everston, Emmer, Worsham 2003, 67).

Passing out Scissors, Paper, and Pencils

These are items that every child should have on hand. If your are concerned that students do not know how to use scissors or properly handle supplies, devote some of your instructional time to teaching them. Students can and will be responsible for their supplies, if you teach them how to do so. This may take a considerable amount of time initially, but it will save far more time in the long run.

Continuing to Teach When Your Children Are No Longer Paying Attention

The attention span of a child in minutes for focused, direct instruction (as opposed to the attention span for playing) is roughly equal to a child's chronological age, translated from years into minutes. For example, a five year old has an instructional attention span of about five minutes; a six year old, six minutes; and so on. Once you reach an age group's limit, change to an activity that will engage the children actively (Jensen 1995). For example, physically moving from the floor to desks, or vice versa; or engaging in a favorite song, chant, or movement-oriented activity. If you choose to continue teaching beyond students' attention limits, you run the risk of setting students up for boredom or misbehavior.

Efficiency and Effectiveness Task

Return to the To Do Lists you completed at the beginning of this chapter. After reading through the strategies and suggestions in this section, review the lists and all the notes you made about rearranging or modifying tasks. How much instructional time do you think you will gain by making modifications to your schedule? In a different color pen, note which changes you would like to implement immediately and which you would like to implement the following school year.

Chapter 3

Organizing for Assessment

Most researchers agree that assessment should inform instruction (Fountas and Pinnell 1996); therefore, teachers should use assessment to plan for and to evaluate instruction, both in the short and long term. Assessment practices are much more effective when they are woven successfully into the curriculum (Fisher 1991). It is not an efficient use of instructional time to teach children something they already know or to try and bring them to understand something they are not yet ready to learn.

Effective literacy teachers assess their students on an ongoing basis, using both formal and informal assessment tools. "A multidimensional system provides the best chance to collect reliable and valid information on children's progress. The system should include both formal and informal measures; for example, a teacher might combine anecdotal records, lists of books read, running records taken every two or three weeks, a writing sample, and a criterion-referenced standardized test" (Fountas and Pinnell 1996, p. 76).

Recognizing the importance of assessment for instructional purposes is one thing, managing to organize for it and to incorporate it into an already busy day is another issue altogether.

I will never forget the frenzied state the entire teaching staff was reduced to during my introduction to report card time. I, along with my peers, spent days frantically trying to locate, collect, and record last minute data, and then worked almost around the clock to complete report cards. After dealing with this nightmarish system only once, I had had enough. I was quick to realize that there must be a more purposeful and efficient way of collecting, recording, and storing information, and I have since discovered a number of ways to do so.

Informal Assessment

There are countless opportunities within the school day for effective teachers to engage in informal assessment, collecting information that results in informed instructional decisions. A teacher is wise to seek out these opportunities and capitalize on them. Following are several suggestions for capturing such valuable opportunities.

Anecdotal Records: Why Every Teacher Needs a Remote Car Starter

"Assessment happens all the time, in many contexts—and often when we may least expect it" (Hindley 1996, 136). It is for this very reason that effective teachers must have a well-operating system in place for noting and recording student behaviors that occur outside of formal assessment situations.

No matter how stellar teachers' internal memory devices are, there is no way they can remember all of the important behaviors and displays of learning (academic, social, physical, and behavioral) that students provide on a daily basis. Teachers must first recognize the need for a comfortable system to record such anecdotal observations, and then they must designate time in their schedules to make and record their observations. It is important to have a system in place for both observing and recording (Education Department of South Australia 1991).

I first learned the importance of an accurate and detailed anecdotal record-keeping system as I settled into my first set of parent-teacher conferences and came to a horrible realization: I had nothing to say about my students. I found myself making general comments such as "She's a joy to have in class" or "He's progressing quite nicely." Or some other equally ambiguous statement, before suggesting to the parents that they hurry on so that they would not be late for their next conference—never mind that our conference still had eighteen minutes left. My comments on students with problems I needed to address were equally pathetic. I would suggest, "She misbehaves constantly" but was completely unable to document any specific instances. Nor could I point out anything the child had done right. At other times, I would generalize "bad" behavior as developmental. I would say "He'll grow out of it" and pray.

Finding a Recording System: Flip Cards, Computer Labels, and Sticky Notes

Three very functional methods of recording observations include using flip cards, computer labels, or sticky notes. It is important to pick a recording system that works best for you.

The flip card method is a simple system for recording and maintaining accurate notes. The system consists of a clipboard and index cards. Label a separate index card with each student's name at the bottom of the card, and then stagger and tape the top edge of the cards onto a clipboard, leaving the names visible. Take notes, adding the date, on the index cards as you make observations. As each card is filled, remove it, file it away, and replace it with a new one.

To ensure that you make observations of all your students, it is a good idea to make a small tally mark next to the child's name every time you make a record.

A variation of the flip card method is to use the same clipboard, only this time, cover it with a sheet of computer labels. At the beginning of the week, write a student's name on each sticker and then take notes on the stickers as you make observations throughout the week. When a sticker is full, you can easily transfer it to each student's folder.

You can also use sticky notes on a clipboard similar to the flip cards and computer labels. Consider placing five to six large sticky notes on a clipboard. Record the names of students you want to observe that day on each sticky note and take notes throughout the day. By observing a different set of students every day, you can collect informal assessment data on every student by the end of the week.

Scheduling Time to Record Observations

Not only is it important to identify the recording system that will work best for you, it is equally (if not more) important to make sure that you have designated the time you will need to record your observations.

When I first set up a system to take anecdotal notes, I would go days without ever taking a single note. It was about this time that my faithful car took its last breath and forced me to begin my search for a replacement. I found my new car and the solution to my assessment problem at the same time!

Believe it or not, the best thing I ever did to assist in my anecdotal record keeping was to buy an automatic car starter. That's right, an automatic car starter. As I was picking out features for my new car, I fell in love with the automatic car start feature. Just think—I could stand in my apartment, start my car, and let it warm up for five minutes before I even stepped foot outside. A wise purchase for a warm-blooded soul living in Chicago, but one that I could not justify to myself until I made myself a deal.

At the end of every school day, I decided that I would point, aim, and click. My car would start to hum away, while I, living up to the promise I made myself, would sit down and take four or five minutes to jot down anecdotal notes about my students. It was easy to record information about the Leader of the Day—a constant presence during the day. I also found that I could easily make notes about the table group I worked with for writing purposes that day or children from a reading group I met with. As soon as I wrote a comment about one student, I found several more rocketing through my mind. Within weeks, this recording time had become a habit. Long after the snows melted away, I continued to end my day, sitting down at the desk of the Leader of the Day (for perspective) and recording all that I had learned about my students that day. Focusing first on the Leader of the Day ensured me that over a month or so, I would have the opportunity to collect incredible amounts of data on every child in my classroom.

Recording observations regularly will make conferences with parents or staffing meetings a breeze. You will be able to begin a conference identifying specific instances of learning for each child, ensuring the parents or special services team that you know this child well. You can then focus on any areas of concern you have. If your observations are precise and plentiful, the needs of your students will almost always be addressed promptly and with ease.

You do not necessarily need an automatic car starter to be successful in your anecdotal note taking. However, it is important to schedule a specific time each day to reflect on your assessment routines and take notes on each student.

Efficiency and Effectiveness Task

To ensure success with anecdotal note taking, identify a recording system you want to use. Then designate some time to make those observations. You may choose to take notes as the last task you do before the end of the day, or you may choose to start your day recording notes from the previous day. Whichever timeframe you choose, make sure it's one you can do every day. If you find that you start off strong but lag off, then try either a different recording system or a different time to take notes. Remember, it is important to find a system that works well for you.

Assessment During Small Reading Groups

Working with small groups of students provides teachers with regular and powerful opportunities to make and record observations on students' literacy development. These notes are invaluable in choosing texts, determining teaching points, and communicating with parents.

Begin every reading group by asking one child to read the previous session's text as you take a running record while the other children are busy reading other old favorites. Also, make sure to have a "focus child" in every reading group. Take notes on all the children, but take care to have the focus child right next to you so you can make more accurate observations about him or her. The next day, focus on a different child, ensuring that across several sessions, you have had the opportunity to observe each child closely.

Small Reading Group Notes — Lesson plans for the week of: 10/21 to 10/25. Group: #2

Monday	Tuesday	Wednesday	Thursday	Friday
Text: *I like Dogs!*	Text:	Text: *My Camera*	Text: *My Camera*	Text: *Do Penguins Have Fur?*
Planned Teaching Points: · 1:1 match · cross check picture + word · "the"	Planned Teaching Points:	Planned Teaching Points: · cross check picture + word · look → took	Planned Teaching Points: · cross check · reading with expression	Planned Teaching Points: · ? · non-fiction feature-index · cross-checking
Notes: · good text level · talked about bold print	Notes:	Notes: · text a little too hard · revisit tomorrow	Notes: · Good to revisit, but this text level is too hard	Notes: · They loved the book, but NF is too hard. Do NF at a lower level.

Anecdotal notes on students:

Student: JULIE 10/23 - got look + took and transferred to mad - "I know that 'd-a-d' is 'dad', so m-a-d is 'mad!' "	Student: KIRSTEN 10/21 - dirty wet 10/23 - absent 10/24 - absent 10/25 - pulled in background knowledge about each animal	Student: JUAN 10/21 - laughed at end 10/23 - broke down, over-relying on phonics 10/24 - evidence of cross-checking	Student: SHAWNA 10/21 - reading w/ expression 10/23 - reading word by word, too hard 10/25 - how does she know about indexes? She loved NF!	Student: KIM 10/21 - laughed at sister "My mom does that. She'd be mad too!" 10/25 spikes quills

Refer to the Small Reading Group Notes (see appendix for full blackline master) for an example of an easy system to implement. Record your general notes for each lesson on the corresponding day, and fill in the lower boxes with students names and notes you take as you observe your children reading. Keeping these forms on a clipboard (one for each reading group) will allow you to monitor progress throughout the year.

Student Writing Assessments

"In their writing workshops, we advise teachers to teach the writer not the writing. We say, 'If you intervene in such a way that the writing gets better but the writer learns nothing that he can use on another day or another piece, you've gained little. We need to teach the writer strategies that he can use on future days, in future writing' " (Calkins, Montgomery, Santman 1998, 105). Writing conferences are both an assessment and instructional opportunity teachers engage in on an ongoing basis.

Initially, my writing assessment consisted of collecting my students' writing and then marking up their papers, indicating everything that they had done wrong. I would finish off what I considered to be quality assessment by adding on one of many irrelevant comments that I had found in a teacher's book of authentic comments to write on students' papers. "Way to go!" "Good job!" "Nice effort!" Exceptional work received the same comments, only I would add a comma and the child's name before the exclamation point.

It was not a very productive use of my time, and I am horrified today to think of how I made those children feel. They did the best they could, and the only response I made was to point out all their errors. In my defense, I thought I was helping them. After all, how else would they learn what to do if I did not tell them? I was afraid that if I did not point out all the errors, that they might have been repeated.

A more beneficial assessment for students is to focus on a child's strengths and to choose a few areas to work on and improve at one time, rather than to try to "fix" everything at once. Two systems that will assist teachers in assessing writing and coordinating productive conferences are Sandwich Cookie Conferences and a simple T-diagram labeled "I'm learning to…" and "I can… ."

Sandwich Cookie Conferences

A sandwich cookie makes a great metaphor for how to make conferencing with students about their writing manageable. Sandwich cookies come in many varieties but only two sizes: regular or double stuffed. If you attempt to make the sandwich cookie too large by adding more filling, it falls apart—the same is true of writing conferences.

Begin every conference with a "cookie wafer." Direct the child's attention to something specific in his or her writing that he or she has done well. This will start the conference on a good note and reinforce a positive aspect of the child's writing. Add "cream filling" in the form of one or two teaching points (remember, sandwich cookies only come in regular or double stuffed). Make the teaching point(s), related to content or mechanics, very focused and specific, highlighting elements of that child's writing that he or she needs to direct attention to. If you try to add more "cream filling" by covering too many teaching points, the conference will fall apart and the child will gain little or nothing from it. Close the conference with another "cookie wafer" or something else that child did well. Again, be very specific so that the child is aware of that strength and will continue to incorporate it into his or her writing.

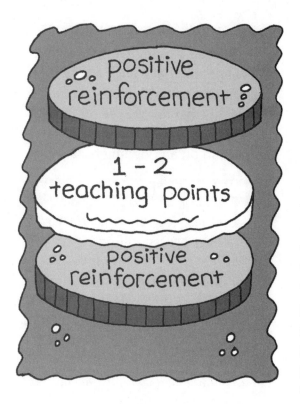

I'm Learning To.../I Can... T-Diagram

Another way to assess student writing is to document the teaching points addressed in a writing conference, using a simple T-diagram. On the left-hand side of the diagram, record "I am learning to..." and on the right-hand side record "I can...." You can then glue or staple this document into the inside front cover of students' writing journals, notebooks, or folders.

I'm Learning To . . . / I Can . . .	
Name Bobby	
I'm learning to . . .	**I can . . .**
9/10 leave spaces between words	9/16 leave spaces!
9/16 stretch out words (9/24, 9/30)	9/30 stretch out words!
9/16 put periods at the end of sentences (9/24)	9/24 use periods!
9/30 use the word wall	

As you conference with a child, refer to the T-diagram as you address different teaching points. As you identify something for that child to work on, jot it down in simple terms in the "I'm learning to..." column, along with the date. Use this form with beginning writers to document the content of the conference, and use this form with more accomplished writers to create a customized editing checklist.

Refer to the "I'm learning to..." column at your next conference with that child and use that, in part, to guide your conversation. If the child has demonstrated over several pieces of writing that he or she has mastered that skill, celebrate that fact, and record it in the "I can...." column.

Refer to the example of a I'm Learning To... /I Can... T-Diagram (see the appendix for a full blackline master).

Hooray! Hooray! We Conference Today: Table Group Conferences

Even though you will conference with numerous children every day, you will not be able to conference with *all* of your students every day. Make sure you do not focus only on the prolific writers who constantly seek you out or the sleeve-tugging students who are constantly in need of assistance. Instead, try to focus on one table group per day.

You may want to create a small chart titled, "HOORAY! HOORAY! We conference today!" On the top of the chart, tape paper clips that can hold colored cards, each one representing one of the table groups in your classroom. Introduce the poster to students, showing them how it will work with one table every day for conferences. Ask students to look to their peers for assistance when you are unavailable. Every day, flip over the card (or have the Leader of the Day flip it over) and identify which group you will work with. Try not to assign each group to a day of the week as there are uneven numbers of Mondays and Fridays, and some days, assemblies or specials take away time normally dedicated to writing. This structure will ensure that all students receive their fair share of writing instruction. You will also find that as students look to their peers for assistance, you have more focused time in the conferences.

Formal Assessment

To be effective in making instructional decisions on a regular basis, teachers have to know exactly what it is that students already know and what they need to learn. Formal assessments not only inform instruction, they are also tools to report students' learning to parents, administrators, and policy makers. Formal assessments are more than just report cards and standardized tests; they also include assessment tools such as running records and checklists.

Report Cards

The teaching staff at the Manhattan New School in New York City struggles with the same concerns many teachers hold about report cards:

How can teachers record the complicated process of learning, recognizing student growth at so many different points on the learning continuum, when they are limited by a document that uses a single letter to represent the volumes of learning children have done? The answer may be just as Joan Servis (1999) suggested when she shared that she attempts "to give them [report cards] some validity through rubrics and other self-assessment tools" (113). A report card is but one element in a complex web of assessment tools that provides a profile of a student.

> The Board of Education report card wouldn't work for us. It did not reflect what we believed to be important about students' academic and social growth. We know that learning is fascinating, complicated stuff. But the report card set out vague categories and, by limiting the number of assessment areas, gave the impression that learning is easy. (Hindley 1996, 136–137)

A rubric is a device that teachers can use to create specific criteria for learning. For example, for an item on a kindergarten report card stating: "Identifies capital letters," teachers may want to establish a rubric stating that identifying all 26 or more would receive an A; identifying 20–25 receives a B; identifying 15–19 receives a C; and so on. Establishing rubrics such as this one not only enables teachers to assign grades more easily, but it also provides students and parents with clear explanations of grades. It would be wise for teachers to consider working together with grade level, school, or district teams to come up with rubrics for the different elements that appear on a report card.

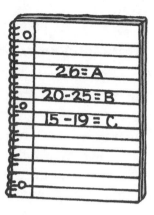

26 = A
20-25 = B
15 -19 = C

You may also consider organizing your ongoing assessment practices around the elements addressed on the report card. As you engage in your regular observations and anecdotal note taking, you may choose to include a "focus for observation" each week, in addition to the informal observations you are making. For example, if the report card states "Uses quotation marks correctly," instead of trying to assess all of your students at report card time, indicate that as a "focus for observation" for yourself for one week, and record student progress on that skill as you conference with each child that week. If you notice that children demonstrate proficiency, you do not need to take the time to reassess this later. On the other hand, if you note that some children are struggling, you have time to provide instruction as needed and then reassess those children on that skill later.

When sending out report cards, consider including copies of the rubrics you use in assigning grades, as well as any literacy checklists and narrative statements you have completed reflecting a student's progress to better represent each child as a reader and writer.

Standardized Tests

Many teachers feel standardized tests rarely give them any information they are not already aware of. Teachers know which students will succeed and which will fail because they have engaged in purposeful assessment all along and are well aware of the strengths and weaknesses of their learners (Servis 1999). Standardized tests can often be a significant source of stress for teachers and students. Even though many educators feel they are not accurate reflections of student learning, standardized tests are here to stay. Knowing this, it is in teachers' best interest to attend to standardized tests in as positive fashion as possible. *A Teacher's Guide to Standardized Reading Tests* is an invaluable text that helps teachers to "live thoughtfully in the presence of tests and to do so without selling their souls" (Calkins, Montgomery, and Santman 1998, 8).

Following the district or state's curriculum should ensure teachers that their students will experience a reasonable degree of success on standardized tests as the two should parallel one another to some degree. Looking beyond the mere content of the test, teachers must take time to consider the actual reading and writing skills that are unique to the test-taking genre and required for a student's success. Knowing that the multiple choice and written response formats are often quite dissimilar from the more authentic literacy experiences a child will have in an effective literacy classroom, it is important to consider how teachers can support students to be successful in this somewhat artificial situation.

Based on the belief in the gradual release of responsibility theory of teaching and learning, it is logical that a teacher who wants students to perform well, will take the time to engage in modeled, shared, and guided instruction on how to navigate this new genre and its unique vocabulary set successfully. Preparing for standardized tests in this manner would be far more productive than the traditional test preparation model as "asking children to take one practice test after another might reinforce ineffective test-taking strategies" (Calkins, Montgomery, and Santman 1998, p.70). Teachers may find that conferencing with students after they take practice tests is beneficial. In a conference, students will reveal the strategies they used to arrive at an answer. You may discover that those strategies may not be very appropriate. A child who consistently chooses the first answer that looks good to him or her will certainly not fare well. It is the teacher's responsibility to model the inner thought processes that accompany test taking, to maneuver through test questions with students, and to support them as they develop appropriate test-taking strategies of their own.

Another consideration is the actual test-taking situation. Instead of having students show up on test day to a completely foreign environment characterized by isolated desks set up in rows that present a stark contrast to their usually comforting classroom, follow Kathy Doyle's (in Calkins 1999) example. After explaining the parameters of the test-taking situation, invite students to determine the best test-taking setting for themselves. Allow them to try out the different locations within the classroom to determine which area will be most conducive to successful performance.

Teacher responsibilities related to standardized testing are not over once the tests are boxed up and shipped off to be scored. It is important for teachers to consider seriously the outcome and results of the assessments. Where are the areas of relative strength and weakness across the student population? After identifying these, the teaching staff of the school (not just of the teachers at the grade level being tested) should take on the responsibility to work more aggressively in those areas. This is not a suggestion to teach to the test—it is a suggestion for teachers to be more aware of where instructional time needs to be spent for students to be successful.

> In one district in New Jersey, teachers and administrators decided to put all their energy into a test preparation curriculum for their students. They followed a program designed specifically for the test their students would take. Within two years, their students had the highest scores in the area on that reading test. The sad ending to the story is that when these same kids went to high school, one third of them had to be placed in remedial reading classes. It was as if the children had been given steroids to artificially boost their short-term performance. (Calkins, Montgomery, and Santman 1998, 47)

Running Records

There is nothing better than a running record to assess your students' behaviors and progress as readers. Effective assessment is that which most closely parallels the task being assessed, and nothing is more valuable in determining a child's reading progress than sitting down and listening to him or her read.

A running record is a shorthand method of recording a student's reading of a text. The system was invented by Marie Clay (1993) as a standardized method of accurately recording reading behavior by noting all the behaviors that students engage in as they make their way through a text. It will take a few hours of practice—about the total time it would take for you to take one or two running records on each child in your classroom—for a teacher to become comfortable and automatic with taking a running record. Once you establish this comfort level, you are in control of an invaluable assessment tool.

Take running records regularly on both familiar and unfamiliar texts. A running record on a familiar text allows you to reflect on your instruction, as well as a student's reading behaviors; a running record on an unfamiliar text provides a pure picture of the strategies that child has ownership of independent of any instruction related to that text.

Running records are most effective when you take them regularly, rather than only at the beginning and end of the year. An easy way to ensure that this happens is to take one formal running record on one child every day. If you have identified a Leader of the Day, it would be logical to find a few minutes at some point in the day to take a record on that child. Finding a time in your day to establish this ongoing assessment routine allows you to take one record on every child every four to six weeks.

Another use of running records would be to use them in your reading groups on a daily basis. As mentioned previously in this chapter, you can take a simple running record on the previous day's text at the beginning of a small-group reading lesson as a quick way to determine whether the text level they are working on is appropriate and to do a strategy use check.

Either way, running records provide teachers with very specific information about a child's current strengths and needs as a developing reader. You can use this information to your advantage when creating future instruction.

Checklists

Checklists are valuable records of student progress over time. The most useful checklists are those that are recycled and reused throughout the school year. A checklist provides students, teachers, and parents with a clear overview of what is expected of that child as a learner. They provide a continuum of teaching and learning that can be used to evaluate both teaching and learning and to direct future instruction. Use the following checklists as samples (see appendix for full blackline masters).

Emergent Reading Checklist

Name _____ Grade ____ Age ____

Knowledge of print behavior and strategies	Comments	Date
Enjoys listening to stories		
Uses reading-like behavior to approximate book language		
Uses meaning of the story to make predictions		
Chooses to read from various sources		
Notices and reads environmental print		
Can sit for a time and read a book		
Participates confidently in shared reading		
Retells stories and rhymes		
Likes to write		
Understands that writers use letter symbols to construct meaning		
Can show the front cover of book		
Understands that the print carries the message		
Uses pictures as clues to the story line		
Knows where to start reading the text		
Knows where to stop reading the text		
Knows which way to go, L–R, and return		
Knows which way to go, top to bottom		
Can point and match 1:1 as teacher reads		
Knows sounds and names of a few letters		
Can indicate and recognize few/some words		
Can indicate the space between the words		
Understands the difference between letter		
Can recognize some high-frequency word		
and out of context		
Can write some high-frequency words in		

Early Reading Checklist

Name _____ Grade ____ Age ____

Knowledge of print behavior and strategies	Comments	Date
Enjoys listening to stories		
Is confident about sharing feelings about books		
Chooses to read independently		
Chooses to explore unfamiliar resources		
Developing ability to retell longer stories in sequence		
Developing ability to recall facts in informational books		
Participates confidently in shared reading		
Participates confidently in shared writing		
More reliant on visual cues than picture cues		
Beginning to integrate strategies to cross-check when constructing meaning:		
1. checks predictions by looking at letters and words		
2. rereads to check meaning		
3. notices mismatches and works on them		
4. brings own knowledge of oral and written language to reading		
Beginning to check graphophonic information as a means of confirming prediction		

Checklist for Reading Assessment

Name _____ Age ____
Grade _____ First Language _____ Second Language _____

Assessment Rubric: 0 = not applicable   1 = rarely   2 = sometimes   3 = often

Observation	Quarter				Comments
	1	2	3	4	
Chooses appropriate reading material					

Fluent Reading Checklist

Name _____ Grade ____ Age ____

Knowledge of print behavior and strategies	Comments
Enjoys listening to longer stories	
Enjoys listening to chapter-book stories as well as picture books	
Reads silently for leisure, pleasure, and information	
Chooses to read independently from an increasing variety of genres for a variety of purposes	
Chooses to explore unfamiliar resources	
Reads chapter books and nonfiction informational texts of particular interest	
Expects to have independent control of first reading of an unseen text and demonstrates confidence when doing so	
Emergent and early reading strategies are secure and habituated	
Integrates and crosschecks language cues effectively	
Monitors and checks own reading with confidence	
Becomes more critical and reflective about the message and information in text	
Expects challenges—demonstrates strategies for handling them	
Is able to summarize information	
Proofreads writing and shows increased knowledge of systems for conventional spellings	
Demonstrates a growing understanding of writing in different registers for different purposes	
Is able to locate information in index	
Contributes effectively in shared writing	
Confident independent reader, ready to go on reading to learn and using reading and writing as tools for learning	

Continuum of Written Language Development

Name _____ Grade ____ Age ____
Date entries. Note progress, any comments on child's samples.

	Date of Entry	Comments
Chooses own topics		
Makes lists, notes, and jots down ideas		
Demonstrates topic knowledge		
Explains ideas clearly		
Maintains sequence		
Attempts various writing forms:		
Narrative		
Personal narrative		
Explanation		
Recount		
Report		
Letter		
Diary		
Instructions		
Captions		
Rhymes		
Vocabulary:		
Uses effective adjectives/adverbs		
Uses comparisons (metaphors, similes)		
Tries out new vocabulary		
Spelling:		
Many close approximations		
Marks approximations for checking		
More correct spelling than [can't read copy]		
Uses correct word endings		
Sentence structure:		
Partially correct sentences		
Complete grammatical sentences (He ran down the road.)		
Maintenance of tense in short, straightforward pieces		
Compound sentences (two sentences linked by "and," "but," "or")		

Continuum of Written Language Development

Name _____ Grade ____ Age ____
Date entries. Note progress, any comments on child's samples.

	Date of Entry	Comments
Adventurous sentences which relate ideas and information in complex ways but are not always grammatically correct		
Adventurous and grammatically correct sentences		
Varied sentence beginnings		
Sentences that use phrases/lists of words, etc.		
Sentences that use alliteration, onomatopoeia, and other figures of speech		
Sentences that use special effects to build atmosphere		
Punctuation:		
Awareness of periods, capitals in signal sentences		
Competent use of periods, capitals in signal sentences		
Awareness of commas, exclamation marks, question marks		
Competent use of commas, exclamation and question marks		
Awareness of dialogue, quotation marks		
Competent use of dialogue, quotation marks		
Starting to use paragraphs		
Using paragraphs		
Editing skills:		
Uses arrows, lines, insertions, etc.		
Crosses out and rewrites		
Tries out spelling in several ways		
Circles things to check		
Rereads to see how it sounds		
Using Word Processor:		
Find the appropriate letters, spaces, capitals, etc.		
Uses editing keys		
Deletions		
Corrections		
Insertions		
Spell check		
Manipulates the print on screen		
Prints/saves		

Rather than using a brand-new checklist for each assessment period, use the same form over and over again. If the checklist is a good one, it will provide a complete continuum, representing the span on literacy skills and strategies that your students will be expected to demonstrate proficiency in by the end of the year. Learning should be viewed as an ongoing process and assessment should reflect that.

In recording progress over time, it is a good idea to use the same piece of paper for all of your recording purposes but to change the color of your pen with every assessment period. For example, you could record baseline data at the beginning of the year using a red pen (easy to remember because school typically starts around September when leaves are turning red). A winter assessment might be done in blue to represent the cold rain, wind, snow, or ice experienced in many places during the winter months. In the spring, use a green pen as leaves are coming out on all the trees. At the end of the year, you might use a black pen or a pencil to record final data.

A system like this one allows teachers to better monitor the progress students are making over time. It also provides a direction for future instruction, whether it is in the form of introducing new content and strategies or in revisiting them. Similar to report card assessments, the use of checklists is much more manageable if they are filled out on an ongoing basis. Choose a couple of elements each week and pull students regularly for "mini-assessment" opportunities, focusing solely on those elements.

Finding the Time

It is important to make sure that every minute of the school day counts toward assessment, instruction, or learning of some sort. The tiny windows of time that once added up to hours of misused opportunities could easily be dedicated to assessment. The following are some strategies for integrating assessment into the school day.

When children are working independently, the teacher has the perfect opportunity to work with students for assessment purposes. Whether it is through observation of work behaviors, a reading or writing conference, or a more formal assessment tool, be sure to take advantage of these windows of opportunity for assessment. If you wait until report card time, you will be overwhelmed and find that you may have lost instructional time in teaching information that your students already knew or were not quite ready to learn.

One simple way I found to keep up with assessment was to have my Leader of the Day carry out my assessment basket during recess, during which I was required to monitor my students. In this basket, I would keep the current checklist or the pieces I would need to do a simple assessment such as a sight word identification task. As the other children were running around, I could work for a few minutes with one student without being interrupted by other children. Naturally, I could not use this time for very intense assessments that would require my full attention, disallowing me to monitor my students, nor could I successfully pull every child at this point. However, there were always some students who had no problem taking a few minutes of their recess time to work with me, others would not take very kindly to this, so their assessment time always fell within the normal school activities inside our classroom.

Keeping Track of It All

It is clear that both formal and informal assessments are of great value to teachers in monitoring student progress and in informing instruction, but assessment may well be worthless if it is not organized and maintained in a manner in which the teacher can readily access and use the information. There are a number of time- and space-saving tips that will allow you to physically organize your records for prompt retrieval and use of formal and informal assessment data.

With writing samples, you may find it easy to keep a date stamp handy. Instead of having kindergarten and first-grade children spend precious minutes trying to copy down the date that you will need to have as an indicator of when the sample was written, have the Leader of the Day do a quick tour of the room, stamping everyone's journal with the date. This also doubles as a way to ensure that all students are on task as each child must physically have their journal open and be working on it as the Leader of the Day comes around to stamp their page.

Also consider setting up assessment folders in a hanging file crate—a small one on wheels will prove to be especially handy. Designate a hanging file folder for each child, and within each, place two regular pocket folders. Dedicate one of these folders for you and one for the child. In your folder keep the assessment documents you want to maintain on each child (such as running records, pages holding anecdotal notes specific to that child, checklists, selected writing samples) and place all other documents (such as other writing samples, projects, or other items that are completed throughout a given week) into the child's folder.

At the end of every week or so in first grade and beyond, take a few minutes to look through each assessment folder with each student. Encourage each child to choose one piece (possibly with some influence from you) that he or she feels best represents his or her learning for the week. Staple the piece of writing to the inside cover of the folder along with a note identifying your reflections on that student as a learner in general or in reference to that particular document. For example, you may note "Julie has made great progress in punctuating her stories. Not only is there evidence of dialog in her narratives, she is also incorporating quotation marks and appropriate ending punctuation inside the quotes, including commas." With the exception of writing samples and other documents you select for your assessment folder, send the rest of the papers home with students.

Using an organizational system such as this is going to support both teachers and students in several ways. First, teachers will have an opportunity to look at each child through a more holistic lens as they review with children the work they have done over the past week or so. Reviewing information on an ongoing basis will also immediately fuel teachers' instruction of their students and make conferences and cumulative assessments on report cards much more manageable. This system will help students as they sit side by side with the teacher considering themselves as a learner reflecting on the assessment tools and artifacts within the folder.

Assessment is imperative if instruction is going to be optimally effective and efficient. Remember, the most effective mode of assessment is the one that works best for you.

2

Setting the Tone for the Rest of the Year

The ultimate degree of success a teacher and his or her students will experience in any given year can be measured in part through what happens during the first few weeks of the school year. Fountas and Pinnell (1996) borrowed the words of the New Zealand Board of Education, reminding teachers that even the most lavishly appointed classroom may turn to shambles if routines for using it have not been established. It is important for teachers to take time at the beginning of the year to establish the routines of peaceful and productive co-existence within the walls of their classrooms.

The time that teachers invest in their efforts to establish an efficiently run classroom is well worth it. Dedicating a significant amount of time to the teaching of routines before children are expected work independently will avail greater and more productive instructional time later (Fountas and Pinnell 1996).

Of course the timelines for establishing a classroom environment that runs smoothly will differ. It is important to base timelines on a group's previous experience with a more independent work-oriented structure, overall class maturity and chemistry, the grade level, and the teacher's current level of comfort as he or she works to release greater responsibility to students. Even the same teacher should expect variance from year to year as he or she works to establish a structure that will allow for successful independent work opportunities. Every year he or she will be a slightly different teacher due to another year's worth of experiences and will also have an entirely different group of children representing a unique set of strengths and needs.

Chapter 4

Establishing Ongoing Routines

" The first days of school can make or break you. Based on what a teacher does or does not do, a teacher will either have or not have an effective classroom for the rest of the year. What happens on the first days of school will be an accurate indicator of your success for the rest of the school year" (Wong 1998, p. 3). It is within this window of time that you can take the opportunity to introduce students to the expectations that you have for them. Rather than establish a long list of rules that you dictate and students follow without question, you and your students can work as a group over a period of several weeks to organize the system that will carry you through the year, making slight modifications as the need arises. This fosters an environment where all may learn successfully and peacefully together.

Rule vs. Expectation

There is a clear difference between a *rule* and an *expectation*. A rule is something that one can break and violate; an expectation is something that one can work to live up to in a supported environment. There is a considerable difference between a classroom governed by rules and one that functions smoothly as students and teachers live up to joint expectations as they follow procedures that have been established as routines. As you reflect on the structures you are coordinating in an effort to support the smooth operation of your classroom, consider whether you will choose to dictate a set of rules to be followed, or whether you will work with your students to establish the manner in which you co-exist in the classroom. It is interesting to note that as responsibility is released to students as they work to establish their classroom guidelines, they often come up with the same or even more structured expectations for behavior than you would have as their teacher. The more students are involved in the establishment of the manners of existence within their classroom, the more accountable you can expect them to be for living up to those standards.

If you choose to have rules in your classroom, they should be reserved for the absolutes, and there should be no more than three to five total. Those rules should be your rules or those devised by your students—not a prefabricated list of rules for behavior. It is also important to reserve rules for behavioral guidelines and not academic ones. For example, "Do your homework every day" should not be a rule (Wong 1998).

You may find that a finite number of rules are necessary in your classroom—both for your students as well as for your own comfort. It is important to remember to keep these rules brief and absolute. "No talking without raising your hand!" is not a good rule as it is not true all the time. Also take care to phrase your rules in as positive a voice as possible. Most of the time, the "Don't do..." version of a rule is not as effective as its positive counterpart. Instead, try to focus your energies and instruction on "Do...." For example, "Don't talk without raising your hand" could be restated to a more positive and true statement "Do wait your turn before speaking." Restating this rule in a more general way also lends itself to a more appropriate application. Students need to wait for their turn in a whole group or small group lesson, in a partner conversation, and in conferences with their teacher—raising their hands before speaking in any of these situations would be unnecessary. Consider how you help your students develop responsibility for their behavior. A dictatorship is not the most successful model for running a group of children. If you want children to be responsible for their behavior, you must help them to do so. Children will quite regularly respond to the unfailing expectations you establish if they are clearly communicated, along with the appropriate coinciding procedures, routines, and patterns of behavior.

Teachers should begin every year with a list of expectations that they will hold for their students. Again, a handful of rules may be appropriate, but if this turns into an unmanageable list, it will not benefit you or your students. What is it that children need to learn about functioning as part of a group and, in particular, within the classroom? Knowing that this may be the first time children have been exposed to a classroom environment in which they will be allowed and expected to take on responsibility for their own actions and behavior, it is

As I think about my past experiences as a teacher when I have posted a list of rules in my classroom, I realize that I cannot think of a single instance wherein a child did or did not do something as a result of that list. I have never seen a child go up to a list of posted rules and check it to make sure that he or she was not breaking any of them before he or she acted. I would often direct students to the chart, "Go read number three!" I would rattle off as an infraction was made. The child would dutifully march off, read the rule, and then go right back to work not having learned much and probably destined to break the same rule again.

I would say the most successful year I had in terms of behavior within my classroom was the year I did not establish a single rule. I bought a poster labeled "Classroom Rules," and after putting it up on the wall, intending to create the class rules together, I literally forgot about it altogether until the last day of school when we were taking everything down. One of my students grabbed it and said, "Hey Ms. D, what's this thing for?" That was the year I had very high and very clear expectations for everything that went on in my classroom. We had routines and procedures for everything—but no rules.

important that teachers support them to do so. For some of these students, this may be the first time they have been exposed to an environment that includes so many choices and so many people. It is logical then to spend a considerable amount of time and energy helping students function within such a potentially overwhelming situation. The routines you establish will be a phenomenal help in assisting students as they work to make good choices. Children must learn how to work on their own and with others and how to care for, respect, and share the materials available to them. It is also important that they have an understanding of some of the logistical components inherent to functioning successfully within a larger community—this includes the individual classroom as well as the entire school as a unit.

In working to establish a productive classroom environment, the first six weeks are of critical importance. During that time frame, there are specific windows of time during which a classroom teacher needs to focus on slightly different elements as he or she works to establish a climate and routines that will support both the teacher and students for the duration of the year: before school, the first day, the first week, weeks two and three, weeks four and five, and week six and beyond. This chapter outlines a portion of the routines, expectations, guidelines for using materials, and relationship building activities that teachers may want to address during the first critical weeks of school. The next chapter provides a more in depth view of how to integrate these suggestions into the first six weeks of school, including the time just before the year begins to establish a solid foundation in your classroom.

Do not use these suggestions as a rigid sequence of events; the order will always be slightly different as the vast majority of instruction comes about in direct response to children's needs. The items in this section are not an exhaustive list. They should appear in your lesson plans, consistently in the beginning of the year and again as needed for review purposes. However, make sure to take advantage of a teachable moment when it presents itself. "Student achievement at the end of the year is directly related to the degree to which the teacher establishes good control of the classroom procedures in the very first week of the school year" (Wong 1998, 4). Whatever time you invest up front will support all of your efforts for the remainder of the year.

Organizing and Managing Your Classroom for Optimal Effectiveness: Ongoing Routines

The following are some general categories to consider when working toward organizing and managing your classroom for optimal effectiveness. These should be introduced gradually within the first six weeks of school with the greatest emphasis placed on teaching routines. From that point on, you can expend more time and energy on assessment and instruction, but plan to revisit each of these as the need arises. You may want to create a chart, similar to the Teaching Routines Checklist (see appendix for full blackline master), to keep track of which routines you introduced and revisited.

It is important to begin with the end in mind (Covey 1989). Determine for yourself how it is and to what degree that you want your students to function independently. The exact time to introduce each routine will depend on your unique situation each year.

Teaching Routines Checklist

Teaching Routines	Routine	Date Introduced	Date Revisited
Using materials			
Managing noise levels			
Getting help			
Getting student's attention			
Working inside the classroom (alone and with others)			
Working outside the classroom			

Teaching Routines

It is important to spend a considerable amount of time up front to establish the routines in your classroom that will result in a smoothly run operation. The more time you spend working to manage your environment effectively, the more time you will avail to yourself and your students for instruction as the year progresses.

Using Materials

The following are some suggestions for teaching your students to find, use, and put away materials throughout the day.

- **Where to get paper.** Passing out paper for writing tasks on a daily basis can cut into precious instructional time. Try to make sure that every student in your classroom has a writing notebook to use for a variety of purposes. Be sure to make additional notebooks and other writing paper (lined, unlined, partially lined, yellow, white, newsprint) available to children as they need it. Store the paper in a location where students can easily get whatever they need. It may take some effort to teach students how to pull paper from the top of the stack as well as how to go about reorganizing the stack if it needs to be.

- **Where to get a pencil.** To avoid the hoarding of pencils or the constant breakage of tips that goes on in many classrooms, start out with two cups, each a different color. Use one colored cup (red for "Stop! Don't use these!") as a depository for broken or needs-to-be-sharpened pencils and the other colored cup (green for "Go! These are ready to use!") for ready-to-go pencils. On the first day of school, make sure each student has one or two pencils and place the remaining pencils in the ready-to-go pencil cup. If a child shows up with a fancy pencil, you might suggest keeping it at home or permitting it to be added to the shared stock as the intent here is to maintain joint custody of all the materials. Several times daily, for the first several weeks, and every few days or so thereafter, have everyone do a pencil search that takes about fifteen seconds—anyone who finds extra pencils can simply deposit them in the appropriate cup. This establishes having only one pencil at a time as a habit, guaranteeing plenty of pencils to go around. Never sharpen pencils during the school day as that would not be a good use of instructional time. Instead, you may ask a child in your class to sharpen them all before school starts. Broken or missing pencils provide students with an excuse for not writing. A small amount of time dedicated to establishing good habits saves far greater time as the year progresses.

- **Where to get a book.** Begin teaching students about the library on the very first day of school. It would be wise to not introduce all of your books at once, as this would be quite overwhelming. Instead, try introducing one basket that holds only twenty or so books about school (or whatever topic or type you choose) all with an identical sticker on the front cover or whatever identifying mark you have added that will help children return books to their proper location. Each book should make its way back to the appropriate basket with its matching sticker. In a few days, introduce another basket of books, each with a new, common focus and matching sticker. It is easy for children to match the books up with only two options. Gradually increase the number of books and baskets, and add to the baskets as the year goes on. By the end of the year, the shelves will be full, and students will have opportunities to visit with new texts throughout the year. Once students have been introduced to the system, it should be easy for them to borrow and return books without any assistance or direction. A good rule is to allow students to always have one book in their chair pocket for immediate access, and three (or one or two, depending on the size of your library) books in their take-home-books bag. You also may want to allow children to have access to the books that are in their table group's book box, as well as access to their individual book box or the box designated for their reading group. To ensure that books are always readily available on every table, you may also want to place a basket of books that match familiar big books and read alouds. Place colored stickers on each book to indicate which table it belongs on. For example, all the books with a red sticker belong in the red basket. Within the first three days of school, teach students that they should always have one book at a time, and, as long as the class is not engaged in a directed activity, it is OK for them to switch that book for another one whenever they like. With proper introduction, support, and frequent checks (multiple times per day, initially) to make sure that every child has the appropriate number of texts readily available, no child will ever have to ask "Where do I get a book?"

- **How to find a just-right book.** Make sure to have frequent conferences with children, ensuring that they are able to identify too hard, too easy, and just right books for themselves—for some, this is easier than others. A good way to do this is by sharing the popular Goldilocks strategy (Ohlihausen and Jepsin 1992). In making a link to the popular fairy tale in which Goldilocks is repeatedly finding things that are too hot, too small, or too soft, you can help children realize that every book is not a just-right read for every reader. Through individual conferences, you can quickly help children develop and awareness of books that are just right. Another method that works with some more fluent readers is the five-finger method (Veatch 1959). As students read a selection with about 100 words, they pop up a finger each time they encounter a word they do not know. If they reach five, that book may be too hard for them to read independently. So that children can always find a book on their independent level, you may want to create book boxes for individuals or for each reading group, containing a collection of just-right books.

- **How to teach respect for books.** You may want to spend a considerable amount of time on proper book handling skills. Use dramatizations, by yourself or with students, to show them how to hold a book, turn the pages, and share it with a friend. Also, every time a new book or basket arrives, look at every one of them with students. "Oh, wow! This one's about . . . Alex, you will really like this one because . . ." This advertises each title, getting children excited about them.

- **How to handle scissors.** Make sure to stress the importance of how to handle scissors. "Your hand needs to be wrapped around them, with the point down. Otherwise, you might trip and the scissors could drive right into you or someone else." Providing instruction here is worthy of a very serious conversation. Role-playing is not suggested as it could result an injury. However, children may need instruction in how to actually use the scissors.

> When I get a new title, I make a big deal about reading the price tag and pointing out what the book is worth comparatively. "You know how much I love to go to get ice cream with my mom, right? Well this book cost $7.95! I couldn't take my mom or myself out for ice cream this weekend!" Children usually respond with an impressed and appreciative, "OOOOOHHHH!" My materials rarely, if ever get lost or mistreated.

> I can remember countless improvisations of alligators as we marched around our kindergarten classroom opening and closing our "mouths" simulated by fully extending our arms and opening and closing, opening and closing—just the way scissors should go. "Wake up, Mr. Alligator! If you're laying on your side, you can't eat the paper!"

- **How to use glue.** How many times have you heard "My glue doesn't work"? This statement is usually accompanied with a hand thrusting into your face a ratty bottle of glue with a tip that has been mangled beyond recognition. This is an easy problem to solve by merely teaching children to wipe off the top with a bit of tissue when they are finished with it and then to twist the top until they see the little plastic blocker sealing it closed. Your students will easily learn this habit if you take time at the beginning of the year to teach them.

- **How to care for markers.** Find yourself constantly replacing dried out markers? Teach children how to listen for them to "click" when replacing the cap. This is also an easy center for very young children, working to strengthen their hand grip. Have students work together—one takes the top off, the other puts it back on, both listening for the click.

- **How to care for overhead projector pens.** Are you constantly frustrated when well-intentioned children mistakenly use a permanent marker instead of a water-based overhead projector pen? To avoid this problem, you may want to seek out and purchase the overhead projector pens with the slanted caps that look like the end of a new lipstick. Your students will not confuse these "lipstick pens" for similar looking permanent markers again.

Managing Noise Levels

Many teachers have tried to manage the noise level in their classrooms by requesting children to use six-inch or twelve-inch voices or by teaching them to monitor volume and adjusting it according to each situation. Directing students to use whisper voices may not be as effective as it is not always possible or appropriate to whisper (Everston, Emmer, and Worsham 2003).

Even if you provide guidelines, sometimes noise becomes bothersome when students are working independently—they are unable to concentrate due to the volume of their peers' voices. It is in your best interest to teach students how to handle this situation by role-playing how to approach another student saying, "I am trying to . . . and I can't because you are a little too noisy. Can you please work a little more quietly so that I can get my work done?" This is exactly how adults are expected to handle the same situation, so why not teach children how to do it as well?

You can also teach a sophisticated group of students to think about their volume from other students' perspective. For example, you could teach children at the Listening Center to check with the students around them as they turn the machine on "Is this too loud? Can you still get your work done?"

Getting Help

It is in teachers' best interest to provide complete directions and instructions and to expect that students can successfully work on their own. However, this is not always the case and an effective and proactive teacher will anticipate this and organize routines to support students who are seeking help or attention.

- **How to handle mistakes.** Effective teachers spend a great deal of time teaching children that mistakes are OK. It is wise to refer to Covey's wisdom once again and be proactive (Covey 1989). First, model how *you* handle a less than perfect drawing of your own "Oh well. I did the best I could. Next time I'll be sure to . . . ." Then, before you send them off to write during the first few weeks, chant together, "Do the best you can!" When you find that one child has made an error and made peace with it, stop everything and direct everyone's attention to that child celebrating "Wow! Did you see what Jonathan did? He made a mistake, but he's not worried about it. He just told me, 'Ms. D, look, I did the best I could!'" You may even have students all participate in a group cheer or clap, celebrating the fact that they make mistakes and can handle them and learn from them without getting upset or throwing out their original effort. Pretty soon all students will celebrate the fact that they can tolerate their mistakes.

- **How to manage too many questions.** Teach your children to ask the Leader of the Day for help or to "Ask three before you ask me." Use role-play to teach students to ask three of their peers for help before approaching you. You will find that you are disrupted far less frequently and that students become more independent. Spencer Kaggan (1992) suggests a similar strategy. When having students work in cooperative groups, they can collaborate, working together to answer questions and solve problems. If they are unable to find the solution by working together, they may ask for help but only by collectively raising their hands—every member must hold up his or her hand, indicating that they have tried but exhausted their resources and truly need help. Using any of these strategies, you will greatly reduce interruptions to your day at the same time your students will develop appropriate independent work behaviors.

- **How to address students copying others' work.** Copying someone else's work is a very effective coping strategy when assigned work is too challenging or perceived to be too difficult. Unfortunately, it is also illegal. Instead of focusing on the "copy-er," direct your attention to the "copy-ee." Teach the second child to turn his or her paper over and ask the offender if he or she needs help. The child should then proceed to help his or her peer just the way a teacher would—never tell the answer, just help the student find it on his or her own.

Getting Students' Attention

Every teacher needs to implement an emergency response type signal that will result in complete and automatic attention. The best signals to get attention are those that are of the call and response nature. The teacher engages in behavior signaling a need for students' immediate attention and the students respond in a way that requires them to stop whatever they are doing. For example, the teacher may say "1, 2, 3" and the students join in on the next line "Look at me!" while looking up at the teacher (Everston, Emmer, Worsham 2003). Many teachers use the one finger-on-the-lips–one finger-in-the-air maneuver that is supposed to work somewhat like the wave at a sporting event. This method may take too long and you may end up begging for the attention of the same children who are unaware. Other teachers have used the lights-off system, but some children often continue working or talking. A variation of this might be to flash the lights once or twice and then start a countdown from five or ten, ending with "3, 2, 1, zip!" While saying "zip," have children pretend to zip up their lips (like a zipper) and direct their attention to the teacher (Everston, Emmer, Worsham 2003). Another method that works quite well is the clap-clap, clap-clap-clap (two slow claps, three fast claps) for attention, which was introduced in section 1. This method simultaneously taps into the auditory, visual, and kinesthetic systems. It is important to practice whatever system you decide on again and again throughout the first days of school; however, there are few guidelines to adhere to:

- **Always use the same system.** Changing methods or clapping patterns to make it double as a mathematics activity will only cause confusion.

- **Demand immediate and complete attention and then follow up with immediate, succinct, and precise information.** If you go on for too long, students will make the choice not to listen.

Working Inside the Classroom (Alone and With Others)

In an effective literacy classroom, students have a great deal of responsibility for their own behavior and learning. In releasing this responsibility to students, teachers must anticipate potential problems and spend time teaching specific behaviors and responses to avoid such situations.

- **What to do if you are finished.** If you spend time during the first few weeks of school supporting students on how to work independently, "I'm done! What do I do now?" is a statement you will never hear again. Teach children that once they finish a task they can move onto an approved independent activity. At the beginning of the year, this may include "Finish your work, then read from your book box at your table." As the year goes on and children demonstrate the ability to work independently in such a fashion, you might allow them to read from their book box or on the floor in front of the bookshelves. Gradually expand their range of choices as they display their ability to handle it. This model follows and supports the gradual release of responsibility that will support your students as they gradually take on the role of a responsible learner.

- **How to sit on the floor.** This goes far beyond "Cross your legs like a pretzel." Work with students to show them why it is important to sit all the way down on their bottom, unless they are all the way in the back. Teach children to look over their shoulder to see if they are in the back or if someone is sitting behind them. Also talk about the importance of keeping their hands off the floor and turning their body so that they are facing the speaker head on, instead of sitting cock-eyed and craning their necks around to see. If the speaker moves, the listener has to shift too. A final expectation is to teach children to come to the floor in a calm fashion and "shuffle up" on the mat, filling in any space between themselves and the person in front of them so that everyone is close together but not so close that children have

knees in their backs. Avoid putting marks or boxes on the floor to direct children on where to sit. When you get on a crowded bus, you do not look for a square with your name on it, you look around for a place to sit where you can fit comfortably and will not be next to a potentially troublesome person. It is important to teach students these real-life skills that they can carry with them beyond school. Also avoid embarrassing students who run to the floor by sending them back to their seats to do it again. Instead, remind them of the dangers of rushing. Pretty soon, other children will repeat your words instead of tattling. With a gentle reminder of "Don't forget to think about how you're going to come to the floor" before inviting them to the floor, students will have no trouble responding appropriately.

- **How to sit in your chair.** It is important to teach students how to sit properly in their chairs. They need to know that "four on the floor" is the way to go.

- **How to ask someone to move out of your way.** It is much more beneficial to be proactive about this and teach it in isolation, rather than to wait for a squabble to break out and then demand apologies. Role-play is extremely beneficial in teaching children how to handle such situations. Children quickly learn to tap the child gently and say,

It has been my experience that students who tip their chairs are usually not being defiant. More than likely, they are bored and are looking for a way to entertain themselves. In this case, I take a closer look at what I am doing than what the child is doing. A child seriously engaged in the task of learning will be quite unable to divert his or her mental energies to balancing his or her chair on two legs.

"Excuse me, please. Did you know that you just stepped on my coat/ran into me/are blocking my view? Could you move over, please?" The other child is taught to say, "Oh my! Here, is that better?" or "Oh my! Are you OK? I didn't mean to . . ." Try not to focus all of your attention on the instigator, as the other child also has much to learn about how to handle such situations properly.

- **How to form a line.** Standing in front of a group of children, lift your arms like flight attendant and say "If you are in line, you will fit between my arms." Quickly follow up with "If you are in line, the only thing you should be able to see is the back of a head." Anticipating that a child will try to cut in line someday, proactively work through this situation by teaching students exactly what to say, "Excuse me, please. I don't think you saw me standing here." The other child is taught to say, "Oh, excuse me, there you go." It may sound impossible, but it works. If it does not, try not to focus on the offender, as you may not be able to control him or her if he or she is in a defensive mode. Instead, suggest to the other child, "Wow. You were so polite and it didn't work? That's really too bad. I would just move away from that person." That is usually the way it would happen in the adult world. If not, there would some awful brawls in banks, grocery stores, and department stores.

- **How to form a circle.** Forming a circle is another perfect example of a nonacademic lesson that is quite necessary. Teach children to approximate the size and go for it collectively. Anyone left out of the circle is taught to tap a peer and politely say, "Excuse me, please. Could you move back?"

> *Other than initially, I very, very rarely direct my children. Instead I teach them to be responsible for asking one other to move. That way, they learn that it is their responsibility.*

Practice forming circles again and again within the first week or two of school. You do not have to do anything with them other than comment on what a great circle it is. Your lesson objective is simply to help children learn how to make circles quickly. You may choose to do a read aloud or some other lesson with older children; however, it is an exhausting activity for many five year olds.

- **How to share or to ask someone to share with you.** Knowing that the teacher is eager to share the classroom with students, students are usually comfortable sharing. However, it is still important to teach them how to do so. The verbiage you provide is critical. "Katie, can I share that with you? I'd really like to." or "Michael, can I have that when you are finished?" Students have two choices for responses, "Yes, I will share" or "Not right now, but as soon as I am finished, I

> *My students quickly learn that this is our classroom and that this is our property, while still maintaining the understanding that this is the case because I am sharing with them.*

will give it to you." The latter may be accompanied with a reminder on a sticky note so that it is not forgotten, especially if you are running out of time. The best way to teach this is through modeling and role-playing with students. Be sure to make the verbiage for asking and responding to one another very specific as part of the reason that sharing is such a challenge is that many children simply do not have the words to use. As always, reinforce appropriate sharing behavior with very specific feedback on what the child has done.

- **Whose turn it is to talk.** Raising hands to speak is a decent way to manage outbursts, but it can be quite overwhelming when there are twenty or so waving hands all partnered with "Oh, oh, oh!" or "Me, me, me!" A quick and easy way to turn this around is to invite children to put up only their pointer finger and to keep it right next to their shoulder instead of waving their entire arm madly in the air. An added benefit is that it allows you to see at a glance who is ready with the answer and who might benefit from additional support or direction.

*I*t did not take me long to figure out that raising your hand (or finger) was not the only method I needed to use to help children in knowing whose turn it was to talk. As I began to investigate adult conversations, I noticed that individuals have conversations quite successfully without raising their hands—even in large groups. Have you ever been to a dinner party where the guests are required to raise their hand to speak? People know when to talk because they read one another's body language and watch their eyes. Children can learn how to do the same. Begin by explicitly teaching conversation skills to students. Teach students to watch your eyes as you ask a question. Then have them practice identifying who should answer your question as you stare right into one child's eyes while asking, "Who would I want to answer me now?" After a few demonstrations, children pick up pretty quickly, and the number of "shout-outs" diminishes rapidly.

- **How to listen to the loudspeaker.** The very first time the loudspeaker squawks, say, "Freeze!" and then stare up at the loudspeaker with the most intent expression on your face that you can possibly muster. Afterward, comment, "Is Mrs. Maloney here?" or "Do any of you own that car with its lights on?" or "Oh, yum! Hot dogs for lunch today!" In some way, react to the information pointing out how important it is for everyone to listen closely. Pretty soon, every child will learn to do it along with you.

- **When to teach reverse tattling.** As most teachers do not want children to tattle, this is something that they would rather not address but find that they have to. With a large number of children together, all seeking attention, some students find this a successful way of monopolizing the teacher's time. Unfortunately, they also manage to alienate their peers at the same time (Everston, Emmer, and Worsham 2003). Tattlers are usually attention seekers or children who do not know how to handle the situation. Telling them to stop tattling is like telling Niagara Falls to stop flowing—it probably will not happen. Instead of creating a no tattling rule, teach your students how to do the exact opposite. In reverse tattling, students look for things to celebrate rather than things to complain about.

When I realized that my "No tattling!" rule was clearly not working, I opted to try something new and instituted what I have since labeled (but never to the children) as reverse tattling. In reverse tattling, I teach children to share only the great, wonderful, kind, and helpful things others do. It took a bit of time, but it certainly paid off. After spending several weeks of sharing sessions focusing on "Is there anyone out there who can tell me about something nice that someone did for them today?" I started to feel that my students had caught on. Tattling was dramatically reduced, but I knew for sure that reverse tattling had caught on the day I found myself standing on the playground with my new principal, after working on reverse tattling for about a month. As we stood there, a student came peeling across the playground, heading straight for me, mad as a hornet. Inwardly, I cringed, worried about what was to come out, knowing full well that my new boss was certainly watching with a close eye. As the student finally caught his breath, he blurted out "Ms. D! Ms. D! I can't believe this! I was just knocked down and only three kids came to help me up!" The "No tattling" rule failed; however, my reverse tattling expectation was an overwhelming success. Even though the student was tattling, his focus was not on the student who knocked him down, it was on the fact that only three of nineteen students came to help him up. If the biggest complaint I get is from a child who was concerned that only three of his friends, and not all nineteen had come to his rescue, I'll consider my "reverse tattling" efforts a victory.

Working Outside of the Classroom

It is important that teachers realize that their responsibilities extend beyond the walls of the classroom. How students act outside your classroom is in part a reflection of you and your teaching. Therefore, it is in your best interest to take time to support students to function effectively outside the classroom as well as within it.

- **How to walk in the hallway.** It is wise to always preteach how to walk in the hallway. If you do not, you will end up trying to teach students while running late for art class and end up just racing them through the hallway. Plan about five minutes every once in a while at the beginning of the year to practice walking respectfully in the hallway. You may want to teach this after your how-to-form-a-line lesson. Then all you have to teach students is which side of the hall to walk on, how to keep their hands off the walls, and how to stop at every hallway or stairwell so that the end of the line can catch up. After students have learned how to do this successfully, place yourself at the end of the line not the beginning. That way, you can watch everything that is happening.

I do not believe that having children march through the hallway with their finger over their lips is beneficial, as I have never walked down a hallway that way as an adult. I remind my children daily that being quiet in the hallway is important because other children are trying to learn, and they respect that.

- **How to behave in the lunchroom.** Once students are in the lunchroom, you may be officially off duty and not responsible for their behavior; however, as mentioned earlier, the way students behave outside of your immediate presence is in part a reflection of you and your teaching. To this end, spend time teaching children how to sit and behave properly—regardless of what they see other children doing. One important thing you can teach them to do is determine whom they should and should not choose to talk with at their table. Part of the reason it gets so loud in the lunchroom is that children are talking to their friends sitting ten feet away. Teach children to talk with the people next to them and the person across from them, and not the kid at the end of the table. It is wise to spend some time at the beginning of the year to go to the lunchroom when no one else is there and role-play what their lunch hour *should* be like. It is important again to teach them appropriate language to use. If someone is speaking to them in a voice that is too loud or from too far away, children need to be prepared to say "Can you please speak more quietly, I am sitting right next to you" or "Wait until we're finished with lunch, please. I'll see you on the playground."

In an attempt at community service, I also ask my students to say something nice to the cafeteria workers every day such as "Thank you for the peas" or "Your new pin is really pretty." Whatever they want, just say something nice. I can hardly walk past the lunchroom door without cringing at the chaos they deal with for hours every day. They deserve some additional kindness and appreciation.

- **How to behave on the bus.** Whether on a field trip or on their way home, students' behavior is again a reflection of their teacher. Take time to teach your children how to get on and off the bus, as well as how to behave while on it. Students should know that the *only* people they should talk to on the bus are the people next to or across from them and possibly the children sitting on the aisle in front of or behind them. Speak to them earnestly about what a great responsibility the driver has for the safety of each passenger.

Most bus companies offer this service with the yearly bus evacuation drill, but I find that reviewing this information is extremely beneficial. I even teach my students to say something nice to the driver before departing. Every year, I ask one of the drivers to come a little early or stay a little late so that I can take the time to do this—I have never been refused. In fact, my efforts have been so successful, not only do my students receive compliments regularly, one time I received a marriage proposal!

©2003 Rigby

Instruction

There are specific strategies teachers can share with students to ensure students are successful learners. The ongoing routines are geared largely toward making teaching and learning possible. The routines in this section are more specifically linked to enhancing the learning potential for each individual student.

- **How to listen.** This is similar to how to listen to the loudspeaker (see Teaching Routines); however, here the emphasis is on students listening to the teacher or to each other with their eyes and ears. Spend time showing children how to face the speaker to watch his or her eyes and mouth gestures. People who appear to lack social skills may often just lack the ability to infer from other people's words and voices. This is something you can easily help children do through role-playing and practice. Ask children to watch you as you listen to someone (for example, when the principal or another teacher comes in) and then, afterward, ask them to identify what you did. They will point out that you kept your eyes on the visitor, nodded your head, repeated parts of what they said, and asked questions if you did not understand. Without instructing or focusing their attention on this, children may not ever learn how to listen.

- **How to think.** Some children do not know how to process information effectively. This is another one of those tasks that remains invisible to children as it is buried so deeply within in their minds. The best way to bring this out is to start to "think aloud" for your children, making your behaviors explicit. You may encourage students to watch how you stare up toward the ceiling as you think aloud to yourself (Keene and Zimmerman 1997).

> *I usually show students how I stare at the ceiling, scrunch up my forehead, tap my chin or temple, and share what I am thinking. "Let's see, what do I think is going to happen next? Well, I can see that this man is going really fast because of the motion lines. And I can see this man walking with a giant birthday cake. If the first man keeps on going he might crash into the other one when he gets to the corner. Oh! If they crash, the birthday cake would get ruined!"*

Assessment

Assessment is not something children need to learn a routine for; they just need to understand that it is something you do to learn about your students. Be very clear and positive with students, identifying what you are doing and why so that assessment is not a mystery or something to fear (Clay 1993). As you take a running record, you can say, "I'm just going to listen to you read so I can learn about the strategies you use. After I listen to you read, I will know exactly what I need to teach you so that you can be an even better reader." Through such positive interactions, children will learn that assessment is not something to be feared and that it only takes a brief amount of time and then they can get right back to work.

©2003 Rigby

Classroom Organization and Management: Strategies for Establishing and Maintaining an Effective Learning Environment **73**

Putting It All Together for the First Weeks of School

Harry Wong (1998) is relentless in his reminders that teachers must dedicate a significant amount of time during the beginning of the school year to establish a solid foundation upon which to build throughout the year. Chapter 4 looks closely at the ongoing routines that teachers should introduce and revisit. The time schedule for these routines is dependent on you and your students, but you must address all of them directly and repeatedly if you intend for students to integrate them into their repertoire of behaviors. This chapter provides a more focused view of what certain time frames leading up to the sixth week of school might include.

Before School Starts

Before school starts, try to get rid of everything you have not used for a year or so to clear your classroom of clutter. Children often become overwhelmed and distracted in an over-stimulating environment that offers too many choices and is unorganized (Bickart, Jablon, Dodge 1999). It is in your best interest to do a massive spring-cleaning every summer (refer to section 1 for more information on organizing your classroom).

> If I am afraid to pitch it because I think I might need it again, I put it in a huge cardboard box and keep it for a year, using it as a table or shelf of some sort. If I do not go after it during that year, I know that I probably will not go after it ever again, and I give myself permission to pitch it. It is hard to let go of materials that I have accumulated for fear that I may need them sometime in the future, but there is a limit to what I can keep holding onto.

Try to start the school year with your classroom virtually barren and without a stitch on the walls. As the year goes on and resources are needed, pull them out of your storage system.

There are other physical concerns you will need to address before school starts. Revisit chapter 1 as you work to establish the geography for your room and consider placement of furniture and other organizational systems you are putting into place. Also consider your resources. Do you have enough books or materials? If not, what are you going to do about it? You might consider creating a "wish list" to share with parents. You could also create a bulletin board featuring a giant Giving Tree, a la Shel Silverstein (1964), with removable apples that each have a needed item recorded on its surface for parents to pull. You could even research and write a grant for money to purchase items that you need. Millions of dollars of grant money go unclaimed every year—take advantage of this.

The week or so before school starts, take the opportunity to send a note to your students on brightly colored paper, saying something to the effect of, "I can't wait to meet you! On the first day of school I'll be wearing… Look for me on the playground. Bring your favorite book to school that day to show it off to the rest of the class." You also might consider including a brightly colored pencil in the envelope as well. For some students, this may be the only letter they have ever received in their life. This may also be the only pencil they have had their hands on or the only piece of property they can truly call their own. This is a small investment in building a relationship with students that is well worth the small amount of money it costs.

Before school starts is also a time to think carefully about what you expect this year to bring for you. Review your curriculum, the report card, and any checklists or scope and sequences you can get your hands on so that you can build a continuum in your head for where it is that you are hoping to bring your students. Once you have laid that continuum down in your mind, it is time to meet your children, so that you can begin to learn where it is that they fall on that continuum. The rest of the year will then be dedicated to supporting each individual child as he or she makes progress.

The First Day of School

One of the most important things you can do on the first day of school is to establish the understanding in your students that this is an enjoyable place of order where learning will occur, and, although you are clearly in charge, it is a place where everyone will share. Keeping this in mind, try to keep academics on the first day to the bare minimum. You have approximately 179 academic calendar days left, and it is more important to set the tone that will carry you through those days than to try to fill students heads with knowledge the second they walk in the door.

Effective teachers introduce rules, procedures, and routines on the very first day of school and continue to teach them the first week of school. …The ineffective teacher is too eager to present lessons; consequently, when misbehavior occurs, they discipline–often without a plan. (Wong 1998, 141).

I no longer include the standard opening activities (such as formal attendance procedures and calendar activities) in their entirety on the first day. Instead, I include the days of school number line, as that is something that I will be addressing and adding to on a daily basis for the rest of the year—starting this on day five or eight or nine would be a little strange. The other "opening" tasks can wait for a few days, especially if I am beginning school at the end of the month and only have a handful of days left before I have to take the whole calendar down and start over.

Most of the first day should be dedicated to learning about one another and how the class is going to function for the rest of the year and enjoying great literature. Also teach general routines, such as how to sit, where to sit, how to talk to each other. Most importantly, stress that the classroom is a community in which every student is an active and welcome member. Refer to the ongoing routines in chapter 4 and use the strategies as a menu to pull from for your lesson plans. Choose the activities that will be of greatest benefit to you in establishing the kind of environment that is going to allow you and your students to experience success.

Balance the more formal instruction with ongoing read alouds and introductions to big books, poems, and songs throughout the day. Remember that these children may have spent the summer break running around on their own personal clocks. Take care to pay attention to their attention span and try to work well within its limits. The attention span for focused, direct instruction is roughly equal to a students age in minutes but expect it to be even less than that on the first day of school (Jensen 1995). The goal is to send children home at the end of the day knowing that this is a serious place of learning as well as being one that they will want to return to daily.

> I watch my children like a hawk that first day, jotting down dozens of mental notes that I will pour onto paper at the end of the day. This task is made easier by connecting children's names to the faces in the pictures I took that day with either a digital or self-developing camera.

You also might want to collect a writing sample on the first day of school. Knowing that assessment drives effective instruction, it makes sense to collect as much initial data and information as possible to ensure that your initial instruction and expectations meet the needs and abilities of your students. Make sure to begin every sample with a modeled-writing lesson, after which, you can hide the text and ask the children to write for you. If you pose the task correctly, this should not be a problem—even for kindergarten children. Here are some examples of what you might do:

- **Kindergarten:** Draw a picture of yourself and write "I am Ms. . . ." Then have the children draw their picture and write if they choose to. Knowing how fragile kindergartner's are, joyfully accept whatever attempts they make. In this case, look for different features included in their drawings as well as observing whether any of them are inclined to attempt to add any written text.

- **First Grade:** Draw something you enjoy and label the drawing or write something to the effect of "I like…" Then hide the text, and ask children to do the same. You will learn if they can draw and write, if they are willing to write, and how much help they will need in spelling and risk-taking.

- **Second Grade:** Provide a text that students can respond to directly. For example, "Dear Class, I am so happy to be at school today. When I am not in school I like to… What do you like to do? Love, Ms. …" Having children respond to this letter allows you to get to know them personally, as well as provides some insight into their strengths and needs as writers. Was this stressful? Were they creative? What sort of letter-sound mapping do you see evidence of?

- **Third Grade:** Similar to second grade, you might write a letter which would also double as a launch for your writing center. For example, "Dear Class, Third grade is going to be great! I am going to work hard to… Do you have any other advice for me? What can I do to make this year great? Love, Ms. …" Think of how much you could learn about children's character as well as their current status as a writer.

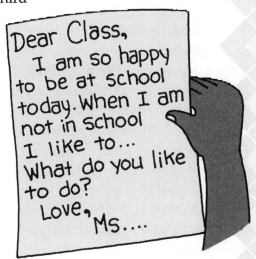

All of the data you collect through these interactions becomes the initial foundation for your upcoming instruction. The writing samples also become the first that you may continue to collect on the first school day of every month from this day forward.

This day has been critical in setting the tone for the rest of your time together. The children have told you loud and clear what they know and can do, and you have an idea about what you would like for them to learn next.

The First Week of School

After learning about your children on the first day of school, you are closer to exploring academic instructional opportunities; however, you must continue to put the greatest emphasis on establishing the classroom culture that will carry you for the rest of the year. "Student achievement at the end of the year is directly related to the degree to which the teacher establishes good control of the classroom procedures in the very first week of school" (Wong 1998, 4). The remainder of the first week of school, therefore, is largely dedicated to more fact-finding and establishing guidelines and routines.

"As the teacher you certainly have the power to lay down the ground rules, but the more you base these rules on needs as they arise and involve the children in reasoning out why specific rules would be helpful to all of them, the more likely those rules are to be followed" (Forester and Reinhard 1994, 160). Make sure you provide instruction at your students' point of need, whether it be in the academic or behavioral realm. Children are able to take on new learning if instruction is provided at the right time and place (Vygotsky 1962). Reflect on the following:

- **How did this go?**

- **Is there a way it could have gone better?**

- **What advice do you have for others that will try this tomorrow?**

Toward the end of the first week, slowly begin to introduce independent work activities. Begin with the most simplistic one—independent reading in the class library. Do not assume that your students already know how to use all the materials in your classroom. Make sure to introduce everything in your classroom: where it is and how to use it (Bickart, Jablon, Dodge 1999).

Once you and your students are confident that an activity can be moved to the independent level, start with a small group of children. For example, have four or five children go off to read independently, while you work with the rest of the group on some sort of whole group reading or writing task. The goal of independent work at this point is not to challenge children academically; rather, the goal is to pour their energy into establishing independent work behaviors. Make sure to choose simple tasks that they can easily experience success with. That way, all of their efforts can be dedicated to making good decisions about working independently.

I introduce many of my centers or activities through a fishbowl format wherein a small group of children sits in the center of a circle performing an activity while the rest of us look on and observe. Afterward, we share with one another what we saw, acknowledging appropriate and inappropriate behaviors. When things run smoothly, acknowledge the behaviors in concrete terms. When we discover something that did not go well, we work as a group to determine an amenable solution.

After spending the first few days doing modeled, shared, and interactive writing lessons, introduce personal writing notebooks. Writing notebooks are more general than journals, which are often used more like diaries. Everything students write can go into these notebooks. You might provide the notebooks for kindergarten through second grade students, but consider allowing third graders to get their own over the weekend-that way they are more personalized (Hindley 1996).

At the beginning of the year, work to introduce a number of different writing genres and text types: lists, labels, letters, personal narrative stories, magazine picture stories, poetry, and factual text on single topics or comparing more than one. As time goes on, students will have a pretty healthy list of forms they can choose from for their writing practice that day. If children are complaining or struggling with the fact that they "don't know what to write about," do not assume you need to provide them with a prompt. You may have asked them to do too much too soon. If this occurs, provide mini lessons and model how to come up with an idea of what to write about.

The first year I taught, I modeled writing every day during the first week of school and made the mistake of never doing so again. It is almost embarrassing to think back to that first year when I can quote myself in April saying "Sure, you know how to do that. Don't you remember when I showed you how to do it in September?" It took me far too long, but I finally realized that writing in front of or providing a writing mini lesson for children is something that needs to be done on a regular basis as they are constantly learning new and different things about writing and need ongoing support.

Start to pepper the walls of the classroom with the texts generated from whole-group writing lessons. The print is purposeful and meaningful because it was created for, with, or by your students. Avoid decorating your classroom; instead, develop a print-rich environment over time (see chapter 1 for more information on how to set up the classroom). "How you set up the room will convey powerful messages to the children. There is no need to spend a lot of money or time on lavish bulletin board displays. A sparsely decorated room with lots of empty wall space conveys the message 'This is our classroom, and we will decide together how to decorate it'" (Bickart, Jablon, and Dodge 1999, 52). You also might want to wait to label areas of the classroom (such as door, pencil sharpener, etc.) and materials. Once the students have arrived, begin to identify and label different items as you introduce the children to them.

As a welcome to the classroom, honor students by publishing their names around the room over the next few weeks.

To "publish" students' names, write the name as large as possible in giant bubble letters and let students fill in each letter with a separate and distinct color. You may want to make these words about a foot and a half high, with each letter darkly outlined so that they can be clearly seen from across the room. Over several days, review the names with students by considering the letters, sounds, and phonetic combinations—all the aspects that make that word unique. Let students choose where they want to hang their names. Continue to refer to their names in the same way you use the Word Wall and make the connection to the corresponding name "balloon… /b/… /b/… /b/… That's like Bobby!" Students' names become anchors and resources in spelling and writing.

> Your name is very important. It identifies and dignifies you. Other people in the world may have the same letters as your name, but as far as you are concerned, you are the only person in the world with your name. It is a name that you can easily hear above the din of a crowd. And when you hear your name, you pay attention … You pay attention because you are important!" (Wong 1998, 70)

Along with writing instruction, begin reading instruction. Daily, provide quality read-alouds and exposure to big books and/or enlarged texts that you can explore with your students, establishing a core of old favorites and learning together to love reading and writing.

As far as collecting assessment data, record students' general attitudes and abilities related to reading and writing. Continue to review their writing efforts as they record things in their notebooks, all the while reflecting on "What is it that they need to learn right now?"

As you introduce independent work activities, find time to start to listen to children read. Try to sit separately with at least four different children each day, listening to them read (or read to them as the case may be with some kindergarten and first graders). Occasionally, let students choose their own texts to see what they perceive themselves capable of doing. It is helpful to keep a set of leveled books on hand, so that you can begin to benchmark students in comparison to one another. Take formal running records and jot down notes on each child as you listen to them read. As you observe their behaviors, look for comprehension, finger pointing, fluency, pauses, hesitations, skipping words, sounding out, and so on. Basically, take note of any behavior children engage in as it helps you build a growing profile of who each child is as a reader. This is also the perfect time to begin filling in checklists and doing letter identification and concepts about print surveys.

End every day during this week, and for the rest of the year for that matter, with students, reflecting on "What did we learn today about reading and writing, and what did we learn about each other?" These daily updates and conversations will support decision-making processes for the rest of the year.

Weeks Two and Three

Vygotsky's (1962) assertion that "what the child can do in cooperation today he can do alone tomorrow" (104) neatly parallels the gradual release of responsibility theory, which is the foundation of a balanced-literacy program. It is important to support students as they learn to take responsibility for their behavior and as they establish independent work behaviors. Not only will this reduce daily stress related to ongoing management issues, but it will also provide you with the time and freedom to work with small groups of students, knowing that the remainder of the class is capable of working on their own for a period of time.

The first week of school was dedicated to introductions and explorations of different independent tasks, spend the next two weeks gradually introducing more options and longer time spans dedicated to independent work. The progression of this will depend entirely on you and your students. For kindergarten, it may take six to eight weeks to establish the routines and structures that will carry you through the rest of the year. In first and second grade, it might only take four to six weeks, and in third grade, you may be able to coordinate the behavior and routine structures in less than four weeks. It all depends on who you are, who your students are, and what you hope to accomplish.

Assuming that students were successful in their endeavors in week one, move to sending two groups off to read independently while you continue to work with the rest of the class. Slightly increase the time frames, from five minutes to eight or ten or increase the number of students working independently. Continue playing with all of these numbers, working aggressively to have more students working successfully for longer periods of time. As long as they continue to demonstrate success, continue to push the boundaries gently. Begin by increasing the amount of time children are working independently, or increase the number of students working independently, or increase the number of choices available to them. Do not do all three at once—chaos will surely ensue, and it is quite difficult to "unteach" undesirable habits.

Soon, your children will be ready for you to introduce additional activities as well as the classroom library. You may want to start with a listening center, as it is quite simplistic. Then move on to an art center, and finally move to other learning centers when you feel that your students are ready to take on more options. Take great care to ensure that you are not offering or asking too much too soon. It is always easy to add more choices, but it is extremely difficult to backtrack and take choices away from students or to extinguish bad habits that are formed when you move too quickly. Although you want children to settle into independent work patterns, remember that time spent wisely at the beginning of the year is truly an investment that will most certainly pay off in the long run.

As you continue working to establish proper independent work behaviors, the amount and quality of your reflective time with students increases proportionately. Use the following questions to reflect on with your students:

- **What worked today? What did not?**

- **What will you do tomorrow so that you do not have that problem again?**

- **What advice do you have for others who will work in that area tomorrow?**

- **Did you have a classmate help you in any way today?**

- **Was anyone exceptionally kind to you? Tell me about it.**

Regular class meetings are critical to foster responsible student behavior. If you believe they can behave responsibly, support them properly, and invest the time, they will. If you believe they will struggle or fail, they will.

The thrust of the second and third weeks can be summarized as an exploration of choices and children. There is an increase in the academic instruction at this point, but it is a gradual one as you work hard to learn about your students at the same time. The print that you jointly generate through modeled, shared, and interactive writing lessons begins to fill the room with engaging and readable print. The children work to develop and embrace their classroom home as you simultaneously work to assist in their development and embrace them as learners.

Every step your students take toward more independent work behaviors allows you greater opportunities to learn more about them as you engage in ongoing formal and informal assessments (see chapter 3 for more information on managing formal and informal assessments). Running records and other pencil-paper assessments are a breeze now, as you have small windows of time throughout the day to devote to assessment purposes.

These weeks may be some of the most exhausting of the school year as you find yourself "fishing" with students: Cast them out and let them go a little way; then reel them back in for a quick check, before casting them out once again. This "letting go" and then "pulling back" continues for the rest of the school year as you continue to release them a little further and for a bit longer every time, according to the gradual release of responsibility model.

Weeks Four and Five

At this point, you may find yourself getting a bit antsy. You have introduced your students to a wide range of activities, the majority of your instruction has been in a whole group format, and you may be itching to start organizing and working with small groups. It is important to remember that although *you* may be ready or feel the pressure to move on, your students may not be ready. It is easy to move ahead too quickly, but you run the risk of assisting your students in learning inappropriate behaviors that may be very hard to extinguish or redirect. The independent work activities found in section 3 serve as a collection of tasks that students can engage in during the time you spend pulling students to work in small groups. The amount of choice and freedom you offer will be different every year, depending on your group of students.

Throughout this window of time, continue releasing responsibility for independent work efforts. More children should be working independently with more choices available to them. You have most likely done enough whole group writing and phonics work that you can open centers including writing and letter-sound activities, such as a writing center, an alphabet center, or working with words center (see section 3 for more details on these centers). You can establish each center and continue to add more throughout the year as the children develop in their proficiency as readers and writers.

When you feel the time is right, introduce the work board or whatever more formal management structure you have decided to use that year (see section 3 for more information on work boards). As students are learning to understand the centers ensure that the tasks are manageable. For example, the first week you have a work board up, you might only have one, *maybe* two, activities that you expect students to move through—the most simplistic activities you can find. The goal is for students to learn how to work successfully within this new set of structures.

> When introducing the work board, I choose to make the tasks easier so that more of their energy can be focused on aligning themselves to the structure I am asking them to function within. In kindergarten, I start with only one group on the work board at a time, and keep the rest with me. In first grade, I may start with all children working independently, but four out of the five groups are probably working on the same activity—usually book boxes.

The next week, you can add another layer to the work board, extend the choices, or lengthen the work time but not all three at once. Increase the degree of challenge the tasks pose only after children have demonstrated that they are capable of working within the boundaries of the system you have put in place. Once this system has had its kinks worked out (through time, dialogue, and problem-solving with the students), you are ready to pull your guided-reading groups together.

It may take up to week six or beyond to get things up and running to this degree. Until then, most of your instructional time continues to be dedicated to whole group activities and assessment. Whole group writing leads to significant amounts of print being added to the walls, and reading strategies continue to be unveiled through the daily read-aloud and shared-reading sessions.

Assessments from weeks two and three as well as any other assessment systems you have put into place (see chapter 3) allow you to begin to formulate your groups that you will hopefully start to pull soon. In organizing for guided-reading instruction, the first thing to do is divide a piece of paper into somewhere between four and eight boxes. Each box gets labeled with a developmental reading stage. Depending on the grade level and population, you can label the boxes with a handful of the following terms (see chapter 3 for more information):

- **Pre-emergent**

- **Emergent** (You might even break this down into Emergent 1, 2, and 3 or Pre-emergent/ Emergent and Emergent/Early.)

- **Early** (You can break this down in the same fashion as the Emergent level.)

- **Transitional**

- **Fluent** (You can break this down by more specific needs. For example, you may organize a group to support students who have an overreliance on phonics or a group of students that read fluently but do not comprehend what they are reading.)

After organizing this informal classroom reading profile, note the month on the top of the sheet and categorize your students' names in the chart to the best of your ability (repeat this at the onset of every month during the school year as a record of class and individual progress). Before week six, you will need to use running records or other slightly more formal assessment tools to fine-tune your estimates.

Week Six and Beyond

Finally, you arrive at week six (or week four or five or seven or eight, depending on your particular situation this year). At this point, you can begin to pull together small groups for guided-reading lessons. Prior to doing so, be sure you are fully confident that your students are capable of working independently. You will know that you have reached that point in developing independent work behaviors when you can stand back in your classroom and watch your children functioning smoothly without you.

As you begin pulling together guided-reading groups, start with only one a day and slowly work up to two or three. If you find that students are unable to work independently for an extended period of time, break up a longer independent work time into shorter segments of time, punctuated with whole group reading or writing opportunities. For example, instead of expecting your students to work independently for forty minutes, ask them to work for two smaller blocks of twenty minutes each, with a shared-reading lesson or some other whole group learning opportunity sandwiched in between each of the independent work/guided reading blocks.

Continue to collect both formal and informal information on your students every day for the rest of the year. These assessments are invaluable in letting you know what to teach from day to day.

If you have worked hard to establish an environment characterized by order, you can fully expect that everything will run smoothly the vast majority of the time; however, every now and then children will slip. It would be a mistake to only gather children when troubles arise—it is often too late by that point and some bad habits have been learned. Alternately, it is wise to take time on a regular basis to celebrate the successes and to identify and articulate the behaviors and decisions that are good ones, so that they will be honored and repeated. Taking a few steps back to recognize and reinforce (and possibly reteach) acceptable behavior is something that will continue to occur throughout the school year. It is extremely helpful to recognize this and plan for it.

Handling Challenging Behavior

There is no doubt that effective teaching must begin with effective classroom management. A classroom ruled by chaos or constant behavioral problems is not one that is conducive to teaching or learning successfully. The solid foundation that appropriate classroom management provides will greatly diminish the possibility of both overall chaos and potential behavioral problems (Routman 2000, 161).

Establishing a truly well-managed classroom requires a great deal of time, effort, and patience on the part of the teacher. It usually requires considerable amounts of trial and error as well (Routman 2000). The bulk of this text has been dedicated to coordinating routines and structures that will allow both the teacher and students to function successfully as a community, in essence, a well-managed classroom.

Such proactive measures are desirable, but teachers must address the fact that effective teaching is not a failsafe. No matter how well you set up the classroom, your instruction, the routines and procedures that are the foundation of your classroom, from time to time, students will act out.

The position you take in responding to and handling behavior problems is a direct reflection of your beliefs. If you believe that you are the ruler of the classroom and that order and control

> Learning cannot occur in an environment where student behavior is out of control. If students are running around, defying the teacher, or picking fights, they cannot also engage deeply with content. Of course, the reverse is also true: When students are engaged deeply with content, they are less likely to pick fights, defy a teacher, or run around a classroom. (Danielson 1996, 85)

flow from you, you might expect to have a long and tiresome year. The control of students comes from within. You can set up the parameters within which they can function and establish routines and guidelines along with them, but the ultimate choices children make are up to them. Losing your temper and responding by yelling or threatening will only escalate undesirable behavior, or result in students shutting down as a result of the threats.

Avoiding Rewards and Punishment

A focus on the *teacher's* needs being met through coercion and bribery or rewards and punishment may have an immediate positive outcome, but this type of management may have long-term negative consequences. Such responses sometimes result in immediate success, but that success is usually followed with a quick return to the original behavior. Such methods for changing behavior are very teacher centered and do not address the learners behavior in a way that will bring about lasting change. Effective teachers take time to help students become reflective on their behavior and to take on the responsibility for and control of their own actions (Kohn 1993).

Extending and removing privileges such as recess time, tickets, or points to be exchanged for prizes, stickers, and so on are also not effective in supporting students to alter their behavior. A more logical approach would be to focus on the needs of the student and the behavior itself. Instead of removing a choice or a student, it is important to take the time to address the problem such that the solution is not merely a temporary one but a long lasting one. Focus your efforts consistently toward coordinating "ongoing structures that will support today's and tomorrow's work, rather than planning one time arrangements" (Calkins 1999, 14).

> If your objective is to get people to obey an order, to show up on time and do what they're told, then bribing or threatening them may be sensible strategies. But if your objective is to get long-term quality in the workplace, to help students become careful thinkers and self-directed learners, or to support children in developing good values, then rewards, like punishments, are absolutely useless. In fact, as we are beginning to see, they are worse than useless—they are actually counterproductive. (Kohn 1993, 41)

Focusing on the Behavior Not the Child

The most appropriate response to undesirable behavior is that which results in minimal disruption to the classroom rhythm and focuses on the *behavior* not the child (Danielson 1996). If you look to behavior problems as potential teaching points, a great deal of stress and pressure can be removed from the situation.

If there is a problem in the classroom, look at several components of the problem:

- **What was the problem?**

- **Whom does this problem affect?** Is it only affecting the teacher? That student? Several students? All of the students?

- **What was the underlying reason for the problem?**

- **How can we work to make sure that this does not take place again?**

- **What will we do next time?**

In responding to a behavioral problem, it is wise to view the situation as you would an academic one—as a teachable moment. If you look at behavioral problems as something to be solved and worked out together, the results will be markedly different than if the child were simply punished for the inappropriate behavior. Such a response is far more respectful of the learner and will be of greater benefit in the long run (Kohn 1993). Using the questions listed above, you will be able to address the situation more appropriately, rather than simply reacting to the student.

When I was student teaching, my mentor Reg had a student in her class who I will call Johnny. This student often acted out. I remember him doing something so awful one day that I fully expected Reg to go over and really yell at him. Instead, she walked up, hugged him, rocking back and forth saying, "Oh, Johnny, c'mon buddy. You know better than that. What could you have done here instead?" I was forever changed—as I am sure Johnny was as well.

In his studies on how instructional management affects student behavior, Jacob Kounin (in Charles 1998) found that there is no relationship between what he calls teachers' desist techniques (remarks and reprimands to stop misbehavior) and the degree of success in handling unacceptable behavior. Instead of focusing on unsuccessful, negative attempts to manage or control the environment, Kounin focused his energy on identifying and nurturing positive strategies. These strategies include the following:

> **Withitness:** A high level of teacher awareness as to what is happening within all parts of the classroom at all times
>
> **Momentum and Smoothness:** Maintaining steady pace in instruction and activities, with comfortable and appropriate closure—transitions are smooth, seamless, and logical
>
> **Group Alerting and Accountability:** The ability to get students attention quickly and providing directions or support succinctly—students are actively involved and engaged
>
> **Overlapping:** Teachers are capable of attending to more than one element of instruction at a time—teachers are in effect multi-tasking their instructional and behavior management efforts
>
> **Satiation and Challenge Arousal:** "Overload" results in satiation, which results directly in misbehavior, boredom or other undesirable behaviors—a stimulating and challenging environment decreases the possibility of satiation.

It is human nature to want to belong, to fit in, and to be successful. This is an innate need that all humans work to fulfill. It is when this primary goal is not met that behavior problems surface. A child will work to have his or her need to feel significant met, and if he is unable to do so successfully in a positive manner, he may revert to undesirable behavior (Walton and Powers 1974).

Rudolf Dreikurs (in Walton and Powers 1974) supports the belief that all behavior (whether positive or negative) is goal driven. He has narrowed down the mistaken goals of misbehavior in four categories: attention, power, revenge, or inadequacy. In observing misbehavior, an effective teacher is able to identify the mistaken goal and react accordingly.

> **Goal #1: ATTENTION** Students that do not feel a sense of "belonging" will act out in an effort to gain the attention of their teacher and peers. Students seeking attention will act out, make noises, provide distractions to teaching and learning, and other similar behaviors geared toward gaining attention of others.

> **Goal #2: POWER** If they are not feeling that they are getting the attention they seek, some students will attempt to assert power or control over their situation. Such students may refuse to do work, defy authority, try to take over and do things their own way, disobey, lie, and may cry when they cannot have things their way.

> **Goal #3: REVENGE** Students that do not feel that they are getting attention and have lost their struggle for power may attempt to exact revenge on their teachers or others. These students demonstrate physical violence and/or verbal abuse of peers and adults.

> **Goal #4: INADEQUACY** When all other attempts at fulfilling their needs have failed, children work to protect themselves by withdrawing and refusing to participate in class activities.

Effective teachers work to identify the mistaken goal and then respond accordingly by helping the child to understand the goal his or her misbehavior represents and identify a better strategy to lead to success. It is imperative that the teacher not make the behavior worthwhile to the child by offering attention for inappropriate behavior, engaging in a power struggle, supporting a need to exact revenge, or setting the child up to feel continued inadequacy.

By working with the child or the whole group in a class meeting or a conference, you can begin to explore the roots of the behavior and identify more acceptable alternative responses. If the class meetings referenced in section 1 have been taking place on a regular basis, children will be very comfortable exploring more sensitive issues than the standard ones you focused on in the initial class meetings. Focus your attention on what happened and why as well as on what can or should be done the next time the situation arises. Such class meetings are going to set children on the road to taking on responsibility for reacting to situations they encounter outside of the class meeting in much the same way. Children will begin to internalize the questioning processes and start to ask before they act:

- **What did I do?**

- **Why did I do it?**

- **What could I have done instead?**

- **What will I do next time?**

Whatever the situation, it is of utmost importance that you work to maintain the dignity of the students involved. Publicly humiliating a child is not an effective way of dealing with a problem as it will only lead to resentment of you and an increase in tension between that student, you, and the classroom community. Emotion is so closely linked to attention and learning, teachers cannot afford to violate a child in that manner as it will certainly diminish his or her learning potential both in relation to this specific behavioral situation and his or her academic learning in general (Caine and Caine 1997; Jensen 1995).

In the midst of a major behavioral incident, remember to recognize not only the child causing the problem but also the rest of the class. Remain calm and do not allow your response to elevate to a reactive level. If the child is being physically harmful to others, you must decide whether to move the other children or to remove the child causing the problem. Such a decision is best made on a case-by-case basis. Children that are of such a violent nature are already, or should be, known to the special support service team within that school, and that team will be able to best advise and support you as to how to handle such situations. It is critical that you remain exceptionally calm at all times. It would also be wise to work with the rest of the students at another time on how they should most appropriately act if the situation arises again. This is best done through a class meeting that may or may not involve the student in question. It would be wise to have that child involved, but depending on the specific parameters of that situation, it may not be appropriate or possible. Again, this is best addressed through the professional support staff on site.

For the most part, behavior problems within the classroom are rarely as intense as this, and, although they may disrupt teaching and learning, most behavior problems do not result in physical injury or threat to others.

"Good management, like good teaching, is a matter of solving problems and helping people do their best. This too takes time and effort and thought and patience and talent" (Kohn 1993, 16). Good management does not come about as a result of a fancy sticker chart or reward system. It does not come about as a result of punishment or threat. Good management comes about as a result of time invested into establishing routines, procedures, and thoughtful ways of co-existing within the classroom.

Managing Student Centers

Effective literacy teachers know that they must provide students with activities that will allow them to work independently for anywhere between twenty minutes up to an hour, so that teachers can effectively pull small groups for instruction. Independent work includes students working alone, in partners, or in small groups on activities of their choice or activities assigned by teachers. Teachers need to establish routines and organize choices to ensure students can work successfully without direct assistance from teachers.

Typically, centers are designated areas where students can choose from several activities, and stations are designated areas where teachers assign specific activities for students to complete. For the purposes of this section, centers and stations are referred to as centers. Regardless of what you label these areas, the key thing to remember is that they are places where students can work independently from teachers.

If you dedicated the first several weeks of the school year to establishing routines and a cohesive classroom community, toward the end of the six-week window, it will become clear when your students are ready to take on greater responsibility in working independently. It is important to note that each classroom is unique in and of itself and not all classes will arrive at this point simultaneously. When you feel confident that your students have embraced the ongoing routines you have implemented and are demonstrating the ability to work somewhat independently of you, you will know your students are ready to take greater responsibility in working independently.

One of the best ways to ensure independent work is a meaningful learning experience is to create centers. However, for centers to be effective, they need a management system. This section will help you create a management system that works for your particular situation as well as provides numerous ideas for creating and organizing centers.

Chapter 6

Management Systems

The organization of independent work time depends on the unique characteristics represented by each classroom. A poorly managed classroom that is characterized by a lack of routine will not provide an environment conducive to independent work or productive learning. Teachers must take time and care to coordinate the procedures that will result in a smoothly running operation if they expect their students to work independently from the teacher (Danielson 1996).

If you expect your students to be successful in working independently from you, you will need to establish a structured system that will allow them to work without you having to redirect their behavior constantly. Centers are an excellent way to organize independent work activities (see chapter 7 for more information on centers). Centers (as well as any other independent work structure) need a management system to ensure students understand where they should be and what they should be doing.

This chapter provides an overview of various management systems. They are organized into two sections: those that are more teacher directed and those that are more student directed. One system is not better than another—you will have to choose the system that will work best for you and your students. In the appendix you will find blackline masters that will help you construct the chart or coordinate the system you have chosen to use as a framework for organizing your students' independent work efforts.

After reviewing the following models, decide which of them you are most comfortable with.

I made the mistake of trying someone else's system once. I had used the Centers chart (explained later in this chapter) for three years with slight modifications each year but with great success every year. All was well until I read an exceptional book by a fellow kindergarten teacher who was using a very different system. I figured, she is so brilliant and successful, I better drop my system and use hers instead. So I did—and I struggled for months. Finally, I went to my principal to beg for help. For the life of me, I could not figure out what was wrong. She had no problem pointing out that the system I had discarded was one that had worked for me. "Good for you for exploring something new," she said. "But it is obviously not working. Why use it? You tried it, now go back to what works for you."

With all of these options, make sure to be flexible with how you group your students. Expect that your groups will change throughout the year, and do not organize students by ability. There may be times when you might organize students by ability for small group reading instruction; however, grouping students by ability does not work well for centers. Instead, try to establish balanced groups in which students will support one another and you.

You also might consider not changing centers on a rigid time schedule. It is nearly impossible to coordinate centers perfectly so that every single child will start and finish at the same time. If you choose to do this, be sure to have a consistent back up plan for students who finish early or do not finish at all. Establishing yourself as a center may not be a good idea either, as that would require your groups to rotate within their reading group families, giving them few opportunities to interact with the full range of students within your classroom.

Take the necessary time to introduce your system slowly—you can always speed up later if you want to. Better safe than sorry is a good motto here.

Teacher-Led Management Systems

The management systems in this section provide you with a greater amount of input regarding the choices your students make. Students work independently; however, you direct them to the tasks they should attend to.

Work Board (Recommended for K–3)

Work boards are tools that you can use to coordinate the movement of students through centers that you have selected. Within each center, there may be choices students can make; however, you are in charge of determining which centers students will visit on any given day.

To create a work board, place children in groups and record their names in the top row of the chart. In the columns going down the chart, place a card with an icon directing children to the centers they are responsible for working in that day. For example, the first group in the example chart (Sarah, Caroline, Mike, and Barb) will start at the listening center, then move on to the poetry center, then to the library corner. The second group starts at the computer center, then moves to read from their book boxes, and end up with a center of their choice. Every day, simply move the group cards one space to the left or right and students have a whole new set of activities to move through.

There are several options within this management system. You may choose to have children rotate through the centers when prompted at predetermined intervals, say every fifteen minutes or so, or allow children to progress through at their own pace. Both of these decisions pose challenges that must you must consider. First, if you choose to move children from center to center at specified intervals, you must consider how to organize each center so that it ends at the same time or have a plan for what to do if students finish too early or too late. On the other hand, if you allow children to move through at their own pace, it would be wise to spend considerable time working with the students on how to pace themselves and what to do if they finish all their centers before independent work time is over.

A final consideration with this system is whether you want to designate yourself as a center for reading groups to rotate through. This option is easier for planning purposes, but remember that locking yourself into a center requires that students are always working within their ability groups which makes it difficult for them to support one another as effectively as possible. You will also find that the timetable will ultimately revolve around your groups, and you will be unable to leave that group to assist other students in need.

Initially, you may want to have students work at only one center on any given day. When they have demonstrated successful work behavior, you can start to introduce additional centers, so that they ultimately work through three or four on any given day. You can also increase the amount of time students are working independently as you continue to release greater and greater responsibility to them as time goes on.

In the appendix, you will find a selection of Center Icons that can be used to construct the work board of your choice. Have fun with these suggestions and come up with the one that will work best for you.

Work Board

Sarah Carlos Kim Mike	Julie Sam Zach Cora	Ryan Amy Jasmine Will	Lisa Bobby Jake Becky	Tom Roberta Bonita Shawn
Listening Center	Computer	Handwriting/ Penmanship Center	Writing Center	Book Boxes
Poetry Center	Book Boxes	Classroom Library	Alphabet Center	Writing Center
Classroom Library	Choice	Book Boxes	Listening Center	Computer

Necklaces *(Recommended for K, possibly 1)*

In this system, determine which centers you would like children to visit each day and then give them corresponding clothespins. For example, you may decide that you want every child to work in the library corner, the writing center, and the alphabet center that day (see chapter 7 for suggested activities for each of these centers). You could just as easily assign children to different centers. Give children a necklace and then have them attach clothespins, representing each of the centers they should go to (either with an icon or color-coded) to their necklaces. As the children make their way through the designated centers, they simply drop their clothespins into a cup or basket in that center. You will be able to glance around quickly to determine whether children are on task and moving at an acceptable pace by noting the clothespins that are left on their necklaces.

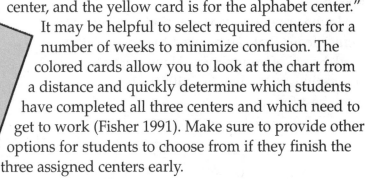

If you choose this system, be sure to spend time with children on how to pace themselves as they move through centers. Simply walking into a center, dropping their clothespins, and exiting does not count.

Pocket Poster *(Recommended for K–3)*

In this system, select three centers and have children move through the centers at their own pace and in the order of their choosing every day. As children complete their work in each of the centers, have them slip colored cards representing that center into pockets with their names on them (see appendix for card templates).

Before sending students off to work at their centers, you will have to explain the color-coded system. For example, "The blue card is for the library, the red card is for the writing center, and the yellow card is for the alphabet center." It may be helpful to select required centers for a number of weeks to minimize confusion. The colored cards allow you to look at the chart from a distance and quickly determine which students have completed all three centers and which need to get to work (Fisher 1991). Make sure to provide other options for students to choose from if they finish the three assigned centers early.

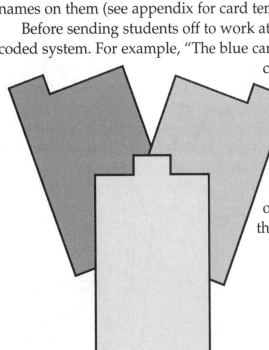

Considerations with this system relate once again to supporting children in developing an understanding of proper pacing. This option is beneficial to teachers whose children work well independently, but need assurance that the choices their students make minimally include the core centers of the teacher's choice.

Center Chart (Recommended for K–3)

This method provides a healthy balance between teacher direction and student choice. The Center Groups chart identifies which colored shape represents which center (see appendix for full blackline master). You may want to laminate a copy and write names onto each shape so that it can be changed and reused every month or so.

The Center Groups chart identifies which group will be working at each center for that day. In this model, children only work in one designated center every day and then are free to make their own choices once their work at that center is completed. (Rotating through all five centers every day would mean that you would have to create twenty-five centers a week!) The next day, simply remove the bottom number and shift all the others down one space. To make it easy for students to find materials, you may want to label tubs, boxes, or baskets with the corresponding center number. For example, Center #1 materials are found in a tub marked Center #1.

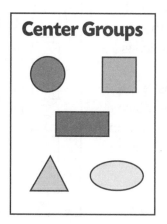

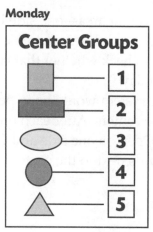

Monday

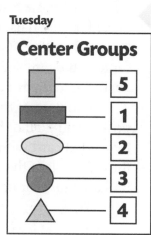

Tuesday

©2003 Rigby

Classroom Organization and Management: *Strategies for Establishing and Maintaining an Effective Learning Environment*   **95**

This model is beneficial for teachers who are comfortable with students making their own choices but are still looking for accountability. By rotating students through one center every day of the week, you can be assured that each student spends quality time with each activity.

Student-Directed Management Systems

After introducing a large number of centers and independent work options, you may find that your group is sophisticated enough to make responsible choices during center time and that you can trust them to work purposefully for a designated amount of time. However, most teachers find that they need more structure than simply allowing students pure free choice. The following choices allow for teachers to provide students with a considerable amount of freedom and responsibility, yet still allow some degree of teacher direction and monitoring of the choices that are made.

Today's Choices (Recommended for K–3)

This is simply a list or a space on a bulletin board indicating independent work choices for that day. For example, a third grade teacher may decide to have students work independently choosing from six or eight centers and can simply list those choices. A kindergarten teacher might do the same, only the list would be more visually based, using the Center Icons provided in the appendix.

Limitations to this system relate to children's level of maturity and responsible behavior. Also remember that for students to have choices, you need to have already introduced a large number of center activities and to make sure that children are very comfortable with them.

Stop/Go (Recommended for K–3)

Another manner of indicating which choices are available is to simply attach a two-sided card to each set

of center materials or center area—one side labeled "Stop" the other "Go." As children go to use the centers, they must first check whether that choice is available to them that day.

A variation of this system would be to post a large poster listing all of the centers. After each one, place a two-sided card with Open on one side and Closed on the other. Place the cards next to the center indicating its status for that day.

Centers	
Classroom Library	Open
Alphabet Center	Open
Poetry Center	Open
Art Center	Closed
Listening Center	Open
Word Zone	Open
Writing Center	Open
Handwriting Center	Closed

Clothespins *(Recommended for K–1)*

This method is primarily intended to help students monitor the number of children in each center, which is often difficult for young children to do in their eagerness to engage in the activities. Outside or accompanying the centers that have capacity limits (e.g., only two children on the computers or only four children at the listening center at a time), place a colored container with that center's icon, name, and capacity number. Inside the container, place the same number of clothespins as the capacity number (e.g., two clothespins at the computers and four clothespins at the listening center). Make sure the clothespins are the same color as the container to ensure they do not end up at the wrong center. As children enter a center, have them clip the clothespins to their clothes. If there are no clothespins, direct students to double check to make sure that no one has accidentally walked off with one still attached and then make another choice to work at an available center.

CraftSticks *(Recommended for K–1)*

In this system, give each child a craft stick with his or her name or picture on it. As students enter a center, have them place their craft sticks into a container labeled with the center name, icon, and capacity number. If the maximum number of children is already there, children know to make another choice and move elsewhere.

Contracts *(Recommended for Grades 2–3)*

Contracts are similar to the above systems as children are free to make their own choices, but they are more appropriate for older children who are more capable of writing and recording their work efforts. Some teachers find that it is beneficial to use these items with all of their students to help them self-monitor their choices. They also serve as powerful assessment tools that can be used in conferences with children and parents in discussing work habits. There are three versions of contracts included in the appendix for you to choose from, each providing the student with slightly different levels of support. Many teachers find that these tools are more beneficial when used with only the few students who need additional structure, rather than the entire class. Use the following contracts as guidelines (see appendix for full blackline masters).

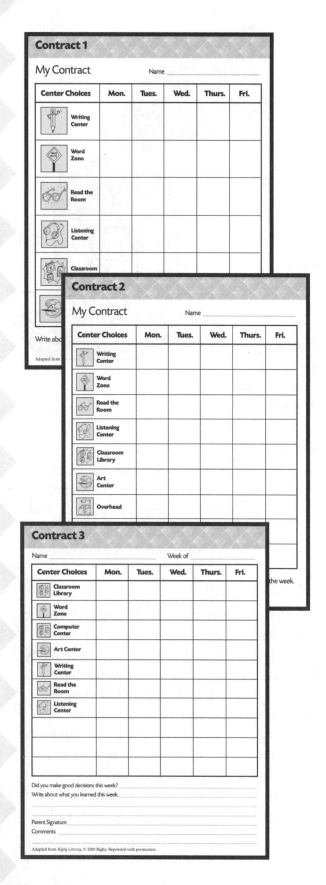

Class Lists *(Recommended for K–3)*

Type up an alphabetical class list of the first and/or last names of your students (depending on their age) in a large size font. Copy dozens of these on brightly colored paper and laminate them for use in all center areas. Children can indicate that they have used that center by crossing off their name or recording the date using a water-based overhead projector pen. These lists become a good monitoring tool as you check to see which children are using which centers, redirecting student choices as needed. They are also helpful for students who all want to use the same center. By consulting the list, they can see who has or has not had a turn at that center, or whose turn was most recent, and decide from there which student should have priority.

Class List	
Antonne 10/5	Keesha 10/85
Ashley 10/6	Michele 10/5
Devan 10/6	Miguel 10/7
Diego 10/7	Omar 10/7
Elizabeth	Patrick
Henry 10/5	Phoebe 10/6
John M. 10/7	Steven 10/8
John W. 10/8	Zach 10/5
Katie 10/6	

Chapter 7

Organizing Centers with Engaging Activities

A well-managed classroom is one in which both teachers and students are able to work effectively. If a teacher is to work effectively with small groups, the rest of the students will have to be engaged with centers or other appropriate independent work activities. Ensuring that tasks are manageable and meaningful will greatly enhance the likelihood of this taking place. Using the management system of your choice from the previous chapter, all of the activities in this chapter will find a comfortable home in the midst of a meaningful and productive independent work period in your classroom.

Independent work time will look differently at each grade level and within each classroom. It is important to provide students with a range of center choices and options within each center that match the unique range of learners within that classroom. This chapter provides numerous center activities that you can use for small group or individual work efforts. Base the activities you choose on the needs of your learners.

It is important to consider seriously the choices you offer students for center activities. They should not be viewed as a way to keep children busy or as an opportunity for students to learn new or unfamiliar content. For independent work time to be successful, teachers must provide choices that

- **are open-ended,**
- **provide for a range of ability levels,**
- **are of high interest,**
- **are meaningful and purposeful to the child,**
- **require very little, if any, photocopying,**
- **do not require extensive teacher preparation,**
- **do not necessitate comprehensive teacher grading and evaluation, and**
- **provide students an opportunity to practice and reinforce both known and developing literacy skills and strategies.**

©2003 Rigby

Classroom Organization and Management: *Strategies for Establishing and Maintaining an Effective Learning Environment* **99**

The best centers are those which are open-ended and that children can and will revisit over and over again. It would be easy to simply run off a packet of work sheets filled with meaningless activities; however, such activities do not help children learn to read or write (Smith 1986). "It will not be productive (or even efficient) for children to be doing busy work like coloring or fill-in-the-blank worksheets. Research does not support such activities, and too much learning time is lost when the management plan relies on them" (Fountas and Pinnell 1996, 53). Working at centers that provide authentic reading and writing practice on students' independent level is far more beneficial in assisting children to learn to read and write (Holdaway 1979).

It is important to recognize that centers are not necessarily a *place* children go to work; they refer more accurately to *what* children are doing. For example, a writing center may not actually be a location in the room but instead a tub full of materials related to writing. Many classroom teachers find that their space is limited physically. Do not let that undermine your efforts to provide your students with opportunities to work independently.

The center ideas on the following pages are designed to be authentic literacy tasks. Each one is designed so you have a host of activities with a range of levels to introduce to students over time. They also require no time standing in line at the copy machine and are open-ended activities that can and will be joyfully repeated time and time again. The students are left to practice enthusiastically, using their developing set of literacy skills and strategies, and the teacher is left to teach.

Each of the centers is organized into two main sections:

- **Materials to Include**

- **Activities to Do**

The *Materials to Include* list is merely a list of suggested items to include. Do not feel as if your center will be inadequate if you do not have every one of the listed items. As a matter of fact, as you start to stock these centers, you may find that you have far more materials than those suggested. In the *Activities to Do* section, there are suggested activities that many teachers have used successfully. Be sure to introduce the activities slowly and only offer those that are well within the independent range of your students.

Classroom Library

According to Richard Allington (2001), by the end of third grade, good readers are reading ten times as many words a day as poor readers. It is imperative that teachers organize a time for children to read on a daily basis (unless teachers are certain students are reading regularly and voraciously outside of school). It is not acceptable to have free reading available as a choice only for students that complete their work early. Those in greatest need of additional exposure to books will receive even less and the gap between their peers will widen even further.

Following are a variety of ideas that you can incorporate into your library corner, providing opportunities that extend beyond simply reading a book. Refer to section 1 for more information on how to organize and set up your classroom library.

Materials to Include

The following are some materials you may want to include in your classroom library. Feel free to add or delete items as you feel is appropriate for your students.

- **Old favorites** (books you have read aloud that are class favorites)
- **Texts at grade level**
- **Texts below grade level**
- **Texts above grade level**
- **Small versions of Big Books**
- **Fiction texts**
  - Fantasy
  - Science Fiction

- **Nonfiction texts**
  - Encyclopedia
  - Dictionary
  - Reference
  - Expository

  Informative: *Description, History, Interview*

  Explanatory: *Procedural, how to; Question and answer; Compare and contrast; Cause and effect; Problem and solution*

  - Narrative

  Narrative account, Biography, Personal profile, Journal

  - Persuasive

  Debate

- **Students' published books**
- **Magazines**
- **Pamphlets and flyers** (found in hotels and tourist information centers)

- **Menus**
- **Phone books**
- **Catalogs**
- **Big Books** (and matching small books, as available)
- **Newspapers**
- **Sticky notes, paper, and writing utensils**
- **Book repair supplies** (tape, etc.)

Activities to Do

The following are some suggested activities for the classroom library. Choose the activities that are most appropriate for your students.

Individual and/or Buddy Reading

Allow students to read quietly to themselves, or have students take turns reading from the same book.

Book Clubs or Literature Circles

Teach proficient readers to form book clubs or literature circles within your small reading group instruction. Proficient readers are capable of having high-level conversations about the books they are reading after experiencing such conversations multiple times within the more formal teacher-led reading group.

Book Reviews

Provide students the opportunity to write recommendations for books they really enjoy. Several well-known bookstores do something similar: The employees choose their most recent favorite book and tell why they like it or who might enjoy it. They then display the reviews for customers to browse through. In a classroom, you might organize a low bulletin board to be covered with resealable bags, one for each child. Students can choose to write a recommendation on their card and slip both the card and the book into the pocket for others to browse through.

Book Hospital

Have a book hospital (Webb 1999) available for students to repair well-used and loved books. Teach students how to use packing tape to repair the binding of much loved books and to use scotch tape to mend torn pages. Books should stay in the book hospital until the doctor (the teacher) reviews the patient (the book) and releases it back to the library. After children repair books, ask them to put their names on sticky notes and attached them to the books. Keeping books in the hospital overnight allows you to monitor the system to make sure it is not being misused.

Parts of a Book or Magazine

Use children's magazines and other high interest materials to provide opportunities for students to explore and learn about indexes, tables of contents, skimming and scanning text, and other features of nonfiction text. You may also allow children to organize for your next unit by putting together a bibliography of resources from the school library.

Take a Trip

Collect all the travel brochures you can find in hotels, highway service areas, airports, etc. These texts provide students with an opportunity to explore the world around them in a very realistic fashion. Students can also work together to create realistic uses of these materials. For example, two students might work together to figure out how much it would cost to take their family to a theme park for the day.

Categories Game

This activity is based on the game Scattegories. Start a file box of index cards, with one section per unit/theme. Have students generate categories such as "Things the Pilgrims Ate" or "The United States." Have students work individually, in pairs, or in teams to generate words that fall in the chosen category. These can then be used as independent, small group, or whole class content review lessons.

The Question Game

This activity is based on the games Jeopardy and Trivial Pursuit. Start a file box of index cards, with one section per unit/theme. Have students generate questions and answers on opposite sides of the card. To play, have one child read the answer and the other one must create an appropriate question. For example, the answer might be "A shape with three sides of identical length." The question would be "What is an equilateral triangle?" A variation of this game is to have children read the question and then provide the answer, using the same cards.

Poetry Center

There are four text types that teachers need to incorporate into reading instruction on a regular basis: fiction, nonfiction, familiar rereads, and poetry. It is unfortunate that this final text type is often destined to appear only during a poetry unit. Do not overlook or underestimate the value of poetry. Poetry is a powerful form of writing that allows the author to communicate a great deal of feeling and meaning, using very few words relative to the message delivered by the poem.

The apparent simplicity of poetry is often appealing to students as it does not appear threatening to them and is so varied that it can be enjoyed by everyone. A poetry center is a relatively easy one to establish and maintain but quite powerful in its simplicity, just like the poems it stands to represent.

Within a poetry center, children need the opportunity to explore poetry freely by investigating and manipulating existing poems and creating their own original works. A well-designed poetry center will encompass both the reading and writing of poetry. The informal nature of the poetry center will also support students in their exploration of this genre as "poetry is a craft in which the first impressions of the poet are the most important" (Groeber 2001, 8).

Materials to Include

The following are some materials you may want to include in your poetry center. Feel free to add or delete items as you feel is appropriate for your students.

- **Published poetry collections and anthologies**

- **Class-selected poetry collections and anthologies** (students' favorite poems kept in binders)

- **Examples and templates for specific poetry forms** that have been explored within the classroom

- **Poetry, rhyme charts, and posters**

- **Copies of favorite poems** that the teacher has written on chart paper

- **Printed version of class songs**

- **Wiki Stix highlighting tape, or pieces of see-through, removable book covers** for identifying features of text on charts

- **Pointers** for tracking text

- **Paper and writing utensils** for students to write their own poetry

Activities to Do

The following are some suggested activities for the poetry center. Choose the activities that are most appropriate for your students.

Individual and/or Buddy Reading

Have students read poems alone or with a partner.

Look and Find

Have children work in partners to identify and label features of text. For example, one child says, "Find all the words with the long a sound," and the other child proceeds to mark each example with highlighting tape. The possibilities are endless here as children take on the teacher's role with their peers.

Poem Puzzles

Choose some favorite class poems. Create two copies of the poem. Glue one copy to the front of a large mailing envelope, and cut up the second copy by words or lines of the poem. Place the cut up poem pieces inside the envelope. Students can use the words or lines of the poem as puzzle pieces that they have to put together. They can use the original poem to check accuracy. The following are four sample poems (see the appendix for full blackline masters).

Poem 1

The sun is yellow.
The sun is bright.
It shines all day,
But not at night.

Poem 2

The queen's pet duck said,
"Quack! Quack! Quack!"
"Be quiet!" she yelled,
"or I'll take you back!"

For older students, provide lines of a poem and ask them to organize the lines *without* showing them the complete poem. Provide time to discuss the decisions they made as they work to construct a meaningful poem, then compare their poem to the original.

Writing or Rewriting Poetry

Ask students to write poems such as Haikus, acrostics, and so on. You might also have students rewrite nursery rhymes as stories, including more detail, dialog, etc.

Poetry Reading

Have students recite familiar poems, developing phonemic awareness by manipulating sounds (e.g., Rack and Rill rent rup...). You might also encourage students to select favorite poems to memorize and present at a class poetry reading.

Writing Center

The best way to support and develop students as writers is to provide opportunities to write often, widely, and freely. Children who are limited to only writing for others, at their direction, and on their topics are not truly writers (Graves 1994). One responsibility of a teacher of writing is to model for children a wide range of topics and text types. Within the writing center, be sure to include every possible writing surface and implement you can possibly get your hands on, and allow for student choice in their topics. It is also important to remember that this independent work time is an opportunity for students to practice their developing skills related to literacy. You can certainly use the items students write for assessment purposes to help direct future instruction or as a focus for conferencing, but do not feel the need to take home all student work from this center to be graded.

Materials to Include:

The following are some materials you may want to include in your writing center. Feel free to add or delete items as you feel is appropriate for your students.

- **All shapes, sizes, and colors of paper** available, both with and without lines at all grade levels
- **Writing utensils** such as pens, pencils, crayons, chalk, markers, etc.

- **Miniature white boards or chalkboards**
- **Stationery** (you may want to put up notes at church or the health club requesting donations)
- **Dictionaries**

- **Thesauruses**
- **Class lists**
- **School directory**
- **Alphabet cards with icons** matching each letter of the alphabet
- **Alphabet strips** that match the class letter line

- **Office supplies** such as date stamp, stapler, hole punch, paper clips, erasers, tape
- **Index cards**
- **Sticky notes**
- **Envelopes**
- **Clipboards**

Activities to Do

The following are some suggested activities for the writing center. Choose the activities that are most appropriate for your students.

Writing Lists

Writing lists allow children to record their ideas without concern for complete sentences or text coherence. It can also double as an informal comprehension and spelling assessment. The lists can be serious or fun—the point is to have students generate several ideas quickly and capture them on paper. The following are some examples of possible lists:

- **Grocery lists** (try using newspaper ads)
- **Lists of items for a birthday, Mother's Day, or Christmas**
- **Things to pack**
- **Friends**
- **Colors**
- **Animals**
- **Things that have to do with Africa**
- **Excuses for not doing homework**
- **Reasons for going to the nurse**

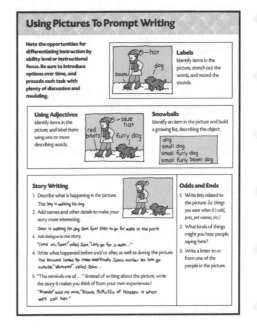

Picture Writing

Use photographs or pictures cut from magazines and ask children to generate a story quickly from the images. This allows students to dedicate their energies to recording a story without having to spend time thinking up a topic. These picture writing opportunities are somewhat similar to blackline masters many teachers use; however, the entire class is not *assigned* a picture to write about. Instead, every child chooses their own. Make sure to build an extensive picture file so students can easily find pictures that suit them. See the Using Pictures to Prompt Writing (see appendix for full blackline masters) for writing ideas.

Tally Chart

Put up a laminated chart or dry erase board that can be reused, and divide it into two halves. On one side, write one statement, and write the opposite statement on the other side. For example, write "I am a girl" on one side and "I am a boy" on the other side. Older students might find statements such as, "I agree with the decision Rosa Parks made on the bus in Montgomery, Alabama" or "I disagree with the decision Rosa Parks made on the bus in Montgomery, Alabama." Have students record their responses by adding their name or by making a tally mark on the side they agree with.

Sticky Note Posters

Write a thought-provoking statement or question (age appropriate, of course) on poster board or chart paper. Then give students sticky notes and ask them to write a response and place it on the poster or chart paper. Give students a few days to respond, then review the responses with the whole group. Pretty soon, you may find that children are writing their own questions.

Some examples of questions you might use are shown at the right.

> Do you think students should be allowed to have common fast food items as a choice in the cafeteria? Why or why not?

> What do you suppose would have happened if Little Ann hadn't died in *Where the Red Fern Grows*?

Message Board

Provide paper for students to write messages to one another. After writing a message to a peer, have the child fold it in half, write the other student's name on the front, and attach it to a bulletin board. At the end of the day, allow one student to deliver any messages that have not been picked up. Written conversations such as these are powerful opportunities for children to experience functional writing (Harste, Short, and Burke 1988).

Post Office

Similar to the Message Board activity, students have the opportunity to write to other students—either within their class or in other classes. In-class mail can be placed in student mailboxes; out-of-class mail can be organized by homeroom and delivered at the end of the day.

Letter Writing

You might consider including postage stamps on children's beginning of the year school supply lists. Children can choose to write letters to individuals or parties and send them via the US Mail.

Class Surveys

Allow children to create their own surveys and then poll their classmates. Using one of the class lists, children can collect and record data. Be sure to have kids summarize what they learned in a grade level appropriate fashion. For example, a Kindergarten student might survey her peers asking "Do you have a pet?" Depending on the child's purpose, she may record "Yes" or "No," or go on to request more detailed information as to the types and numbers of pets each child has. Children can summarize this information in a statement to the class, or they could even record it in the form of a student-generated graph.

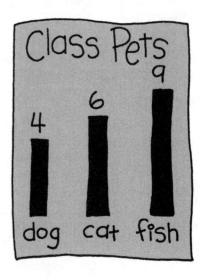

Headline Writing

Provide pictures from newspapers, magazines, old history texts, or your photo album, and ask students to write captions or headlines that spark interest. You may choose to have a "Picture of the Week" that every child provides headlines for, or you may just have a collection of them in a book that children can add to throughout the year.

Powerful Leads

This activity is similar to the Headline Writing activity. In this activity, ask children to suggest powerful leads for a story that might be written in connection with the picture.

Catalogs

Take out all the descriptive words and phrases from the catalog descriptions, leaving the item descriptors very banal, and have children rewrite them. Or, let kids use pictures and create their own catalogs, writing their own creative descriptions for each item.
If you have catalogs that support specific populations (e.g., children, runners, or campers), let children use them as models to create unique catalogs of their choice. For example, students might want to create a catalog for Antarctic explorers, the first colonists on Mars, or orangutans.

Letters to...

Collect advice letters from the newspaper and have children write responses to the "Dear Abby," type letters. Or, allow children to create their own requests for advice and let other children respond to the letters.

Story Problems

Mathematical story problems are a lot more fun when you can relate to them. Allow children to create their own and share them with other students to solve.

Where am I?

Allow students to direct each other from one location to another on a map, by providing a written set of instructions. The first child needs to designate a starting point, and then provide step-by-step written directions for which roads to travel. The second child follows the directions and compares his or her final destination to the location the direction giver intended. These can be left in the center for other students to reuse, only be sure to have students record the ultimate destination on a key or on the back of the set of directions.

Using the maps as models, you might also have students create their own map of a fictional location from their reading.

Handwriting/Penmanship Center

Although handwriting and penmanship are best taught through authentic writing in which neatness is important to both the writer and the reader for effective communication, it is valuable to provide opportunities for students to practice these skills. It is important to catch and correct any improper letter formation and grips as early as possible if it is to be corrected. An excellent support resource for this purpose is the school or district appointed occupational therapist.

Materials to Include

The following are some materials you may want to include in your handwriting/penmanship center. Feel free to add or delete items as you feel is appropriate for your students.

- **All shapes, sizes, and colors of paper** available, both with and without lines at all grade levels

- **Writing utensils** such as pens, pencils, crayons, chalk, markers

- **Miniature white boards or chalkboards**

- **Clipboards**

- **Easels**

- **Sponge tip pens** (sold for sealing envelopes)

- **Paintbrushes**

- **Handwriting models** (cursive or manuscript depending on the grade level)

Activities to Do

The following are some suggested activities for the handwriting/penmanship center. Choose the activities that are most appropriate for your students.

Free Writing

Have a variety of surfaces available for writing practice. You may need to remind children that these materials are available for them to practice their handwriting not their drawing. White boards are especially nice because children can erase their mistakes without leaving a trace.

Laminated Pages and "Lipstick Pens"

There is something magical about using water-based overhead pens—the tops of the pens are slanted like a lipstick, thus the name "lipstick pens." It seems that the usual boring and meaningless handwriting practice sheets that are copied and given to the whole class hold an entirely different value when just a few of each are laminated and used for practice with lipstick pens. You might also try copying them on colorful paper and cutting the pages into small strips to make the task more manageable and appealing.

Goo Writing

Put a bit of finger paint or pudding in a small resealable bag. Have children gently use their finger to write the letters through the bag. Shaving cream sprayed on desks is also beneficial for both handwriting practice and the cleaning of desks.

Water Writing

Use "sponge pens" designed for sealing envelopes to practice writing letters on the chalkboard. The water dries quickly and does not leave a mess.

Forms

Collect job applications and other forms (bank slips, sweepstakes forms, etc.) and encourage students to fill them out as neatly as possible.

Interviews

Create your own classroom information/interview sheets and have children interview one another, recording responses as neatly as possible so that they will be able to post their information for others to read.

Read the Room

The environment of an effective literacy classroom is saturated with meaningful print (Cambourne 1988). As the print that was generated for, with, or by the students within that classroom fills the walls, it becomes readable and of high interest to all students (Mooney 1990). Students need to read large quantities of accessible text to develop and grow as readers—it makes sense to use the classroom environment for this purpose.

Reading the room gives children the opportunity to revisit all of the texts that have been published within the classroom. For children to be successful in this center, the classroom must have enough print to keep the children busy reading, the text must be independently readable by children, and the texts must be of interest to the children. This will generally exclude most items purchased at teacher's stores and a lot of what was on the walls of the classroom before the students arrive on the first day of school. Such material tends to become "wallpaper" rather than rich and engaging text (Cambourne 1988). Who reads wallpaper? Meaningful print is usually something the children have watched the teacher write (modeled writing), constructed with the teacher (shared or interactive writing), or something they have explored together (poem charts, word walls, etc.). Start empty and let your walls grow to be filled as the year moves on.

Materials to Include

Some materials you may want to include in a read the room center are listed below. Feel free to add or delete items as you feel is appropriate for your students.

- **Reading glasses** (Pick up a set of four cheap sunglasses at the dollar store. Pop out the lenses and let children wear them as they read. If students do not want to wear them, they can tuck them in their shirts. By only having four pair, you control the number of children that can be off reading the room at any given time. Obviously, this suggestion is more appropriate for younger students.)

- **Pointers** (Use chopsticks or spray-painted dowel rods for children to use as pointers. You can control the number of students at this center by limiting the number of pointers. You would be wise to spend considerable time setting up the "Dos" and "Don'ts" for this activity, or you may find your students using their pointers for sword fights.)

- **Text Ideas:**
  - Poems
  - Rhyme charts
  - Lyrics to songs
  - Innovations on favorite texts
  - Re-illustrated texts

- **Captions for illustrations** (It is a good idea to support emergent readers by using patterned captions. For example, "This is Colleen's picture." "This is Henry's picture." "This is Amy's picture." Or, next to self-portraits of the children, add "C is for Colleen." "H is for Henry." The possibilities for introducing sight words and concepts about print here are endless.)

- **Word wall**

- **Class lists/ names**

- **Giant color words** (Let students paint or decorate the words themselves. For example, create a gigantic bubble lettered word such as "Yellow" and let students sponge paint it in shades of yellow as a class project.)

Activities to Do

The following are some suggested activities for the read the room center. Choose the activities that are most appropriate for your students.

Word Wall Activities

Teach children how to play "I Spy" games with a partner using the words. One student can say, "I spy a word that rhymes with 'hat'." The other child tries to find the word. Variations include finding a word that starts or ends the same way as another, searching for a word that has a certain sound, or locating a word that has two syllables (Cunningham 1995).

Using word family/phonogram charts, play onset/rime games with a partner: One child says, the onset "B"; the partner says the rime "UG." Together, they say "BUG!" They then continue with the other words, the first child always being responsible for the onset, the second for the rime.

Art Center

Children creating art pieces to decorate refrigerators is a brilliant way to develop small motor skills, learn about unique features and characteristics of different objects, and experience an enjoyable form of expression. Exploring the arts is critical in the development of any child. Take caution not to spend too much time here if the artwork takes the form of coloring, cutting out, and pasting together an art project that started out as a blackline master and results in a class set of nearly identical products. True artistic responses are open-ended and do not require a copy machine.

Slagle makes a valid point here. If teaching children to read is the primary intention, it is important to make careful decisions regarding how to use instructional time. Try to avoid whole group art projects. Other than an introduction to a task, using whole group time for an in-class art project is not the best use of instructional time. That time would be much better spent on an academic task of sorts, moving the art project into a center that all children have a chance to work through. An added bonus here is that clean up is much more manageable. Instead of having twenty-five children struggle to use glue, paint, or tissue paper at once, you only have a handful of children doing so and can easily call on other students for assistance in coordinating and cleaning up the project.

> A friend and colleague of mine, John Slagle (2001) once commented to me, "How can cutting out a bunny and pasting a cotton ball on its behind help kids learn how to read?" I laughed. And I agreed.

Materials to Include

The following are some materials you may want to include in your art center. Feel free to add or delete items as you feel is appropriate for your students. (Please note that it might not be a good idea to have *all* of these materials available *all* the time.)

- **Paper**
  - *Letter- or legal-size paper (Ask businesses to donate the paper they usually discard or recycle. Your students can use the back.)*
  - *Large white paper (Either purchase or ask a local butcher to donate.)*
  - *Paper grocery bags (Collect from your students, and cut them open and use these for big books or murals.)*
  - *Scrap paper*
  - *Tissue paper*

- **Supplies** (Purchase these items with the school budget or ask local businesses or parents to donate.)
  - *Glue*
  - *Paint (tempera and water color)*
  - *Paint brushes*
  - *Scissors*
  - *Markers*
  - *Crayons*
  - *Pencils*
  - *Chalk*
  - *Liquid chalk*

Activities to Do

The following are some suggested activities for the art center. Choose the activities that are most appropriate for your students. Be creative when setting up these activities. Use sponge paint, wash watercolor over crayon or chalk, put glitter in a mixture of glue and water to make "glittery glue paint," or use watered down glue to make tissue paper collages.

Artwork for Books

Have children re-illustrate a favorite text. Type up the words and let children make a class-illustrated version of a favorite text.

Or, have students create an innovation on a favorite text, and then illustrate and publish it as a class book or a mural. For example, after reading *Brown Bear, Brown Bear* by Bill Martin Jr (1995), students may want to make their own version using different animals and colors or children as the characters.

Another option is to have students create a book of idioms, nonfiction text features, or Hink Pinks (Cunningham 1995), which are rhyming word pairs, such as "fat cat" or "pink drink." Each child (or pair) is responsible for illustrating his or her own page to be added to a class book. If you would like for every child to have his or her own copy, consider having children draw the pictures with a thick black pen. Photocopy the class set and make coloring books for students to keep.

Ilustrate Environmental Print

Have children make illustrations for shared- and modeled-writing texts to be posted in the room (e.g., if you write a grocery list over a few days as a modeled or shared writing lesson, let different children be responsible for illustrating the different items).

Do your kids love a poem in a small book? Enlarge the text by writing it on chart paper and put them in charge of the accompanying illustration. This may be a group or individual effort.

You might also have every child in kindergarten and first grade draw the same picture (e.g., draw a picture of yourself, paint a picture of a pumpkin, or make a collage fish using tissue paper). As a whole group shared-writing lesson, add a matching patterned text (e.g., "This is Sarah." "This is the pumpkin Sarah made." "Sarah's fish can swim."). Be sure to use the same text for each one, except for the name. (e.g., "This is Julie." "This is the pumpkin Julie made." "Julie's fish can swim."). This is great example of appropriate environmental print because it is meaningful, readable, and includes sight words. Only have a few students work on these each day as they can be used as a shared-reading text the following day. Having too many at once might overwhelm students as you try to make teaching points.

Journals

Let children draw pictures of things they might want to write about in their journals. When it is time to write, they can get right to work.

Word Zone

This section includes a variety of activities that can also be used for an alphabet center or a vocabulary center. As children begin to work with and explore letters and words and how they are structured, they will be better prepared to use their graphophonic knowledge as they read and write. All of the activities have been designed to provide authentic and engaging opportunities to explore different phonetic elements and concepts.

Materials to Include

Listed at the right are some materials you may want to include in the word zone. Feel free to add or delete items as you feel is appropriate for your students.

- **Magnetic letters**
- **Class lists**
- **Cards with individual students' names**
- **Letter cards** (capital and lowercase)
- **Sight word cards**
- **Alphabet cards**
- **Small letter lines**
- **Games and activities related to letters and words** (such as Alphabet Bingo or other games you may have on hand)

Activities to Do

The following are some suggested activities for the word zone. Choose the activities that are most appropriate for your students.

Magnetic Letters

Have students sort letters by putting together the alphabet or by finding all the tall letters, short letters, vowels, letters with humps. You can also ask them to make lists of words (friends, colors, ect.), create word families (the "at" family includes "at," "cat," "sat," "mat," "hat"), or put together word trains (dog–grass–sun–nose…).

You can also have students use magnetic letters to play the Name Game. Write students' names on sentence strips cut to the length of their name. Add a photograph of each child to aid younger children in identifying their classmates' names. In place of the first letter (or cluster of letters if it is a blend or digraph) of each child's name, put an empty box. Ask children to fill in the box with the correct letter or letter combination using magnetic letters.

For a fun phonemic awareness activity, they can substitute the correct letter for the letter of their choice, creating an entirely new "word." For example, "Mike" would be recorded as "–ike " and students could substitute different letters, creating both real and nonsense words such as "hike," "like," "rike," and "zike."

Note: *You can easily organize and store magnetic letters in tackle boxes or shoe boxes.*

Matching Games

Matching games include having students match words to pictures, letters to pictures, capital letters to lowercase letters, manuscript to cursive writing, and so on. You can also use old flash cards, magazine pictures, or bulletin board borders cut apart to play well-known card games such as Old Maid, Go Fish, or Memory.

Newspaper Searches

Encourage children to use a newspaper to hunt for words in different categories (e.g., countries, people's names, adjectives, compound words, different words for "said," long e words, or two syllable words). When children find a word that fits into the category either you or your students identified, they can either copy that word onto a piece of paper housing the collection or cut out the words and glue them onto a paper.

You can also have children search the newspaper for one, two, three, four... letter words and sort them into categories by length. Children can either write the words or cut them out, but be sure to monitor the activity to make sure that it maintains its focus on words and does not turn into a cut and paste activity. Try it with syllables, too.

Reprogrammed Games

Take familiar games such as Candyland and reprogram the game by changing the focus from colors to letters. Write letters onto all of the spaces on the board and then record letters onto the game cards. Instruct children to pull cards and move their pieces to the letter that matches their cards. You could do the same activity with older students by programming each space with a number one, two, or three. On the cards, write a word with one, two, or three syllables. Instruct children to pull cards, count the syllables, and move their pieces accordingly.

Fancy Words/ Names

Let children choose a word they love or their name, write it poster size in bubble letters (you may need to this for younger students), and decorate it. Celebrate each word with the entire class, savoring its unique features.

Sniglets

Sniglets is a term coined by the popular television show *Saturday Night Live* for words they invented to match common objects or actions that did not already have a term or label. Older children can have fun creating words and definitions for things that do not yet have labels (e.g., the film that covers the top of pudding might be called "shlick"). Encourage students to organize these definitions into a silly class dictionary of invented words.

Note: *This is not a good activity for students who are learning English as a second language.*

Hink Pinks

Hink Pinks are rhyming word pairs, such as "fat cat" or "pink drink" (Cunningham 1995). Ask students to create riddles that other children can try to figure out. For example, the answer to "What is a chubby kitty?" could be a "fat cat" or a "flabby tabby."

Letter Cards/Tiles

Use one-inch ceramic floor tiles and write letters on them using permanent pens or dry erase pens. Have children use the tiles to make their full name (or someone else's) and then try to see how many words they can make and record using those letters.

Color Word Puzzles

For practice spelling and identifying the eight basic color words (red, orange, yellow, green, blue, purple, brown, black), write each color word on an envelope using a pen that matches that color. Place letter cards with the corresponding letters into the envelope. For example, the word "red" would be written on an envelope in a red pen. Inside the envelope children will find three letter cards: one with the letter "r," one with "e," and one with "d." Have children spell the word by putting the letters in the proper order.

> Animal
> Alphabet List
> A aardvark
> B buffalo
> C cat
> D dog
> E eagle

Alphabetical Lists

Have children create an alphabetical list of words related to a given topic (e.g., content area topic, things in the room, foods, animals, and famous people). The challenge is for students to come up with something for each letter of the alphabet.

A to Z Stories

Challenge students to write short stories that are alphabetical in nature. The first word must start with the letter A, the second word with the letter B, and so on. For example,

"**A b**ig **c**at **d**oesn't **e**at **f**urry **g**reen **h**amburgers **i**n …"

Alliterative Sentences

Tongue twisters are always fun to say and create. They also provide students with the opportunity to explore the phonetic element that remains constant through all or most of the sentence. Challenge children to generate all the words they can think of that begin with the same initial sound, and then construct a tongue twister using those words. For example, "Liz loves to lick luscious lollipops!" or "Kirsten and Colleen can kiss quite a lot of kangaroos." Notice in the second example that although the initial letters are different, the sounds are the same.

Alphabet Books

Allow children to read alphabet books individually or with a partner. Make sure you have plenty available, such as *Q is for Duck* (Etling 1980), *Tomorrow's Alphabet* (Shannon 1996), *The Z Was Zapped* (Van Allsburg 1987), Rigby's PM alphabet/ blend books, *Dr. Seuss' ABC* (Seuss 1963).

You also might want to invite students to write their own alphabet books. Young children can create their own simple ones using pictures cut from old phonics books and older students can work to create alphabet books linked to their content area studies (e.g., an alphabet book on the first Thanksgiving).

Modeling Clay

Give students modeling clay and ask them to roll snakes and form letters with or without a model.

You also might try using alphabet cookie cutters to cut out modeling clay letters and make words.

Content Area Word Activities

Generate a list of topic words and write each one on a separate index card. Then have children sort them into categories. Provide categories for a closed sort, or let children create their own categories for an open sort activity. An example would be the words "lion," "tuna," "monkey," "parrot," "frog," "alligator," and a list of other animals that child would be expected to sort out either by habitat, dangerous/not dangerous to humans, or by the type of animal.

You also might ask children to build word ladders by listing topic-related words, starting with one syllable words, then two syllable words, then three, and so on.

Listening Center
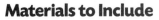

Listening to stories read on tape provides children with several benefits. First, they are exposed to the fluent and expressive reading that they need to have modeled for to take on the responsibility for such reading themselves. Secondly, children are able to listen to the reader as they follow along in the text, giving them an opportunity to match the spoken word to the written word as the narrator makes his or her way through the text as the child reads along. Many of the audiotapes available include music, songs, and activities related to the text that will further engage students.

Don Holdaway (1979) makes an interesting point about the audiotapes used in listening centers, "We use mainly male voices because many of the slower children are boys and they must not get the idea that reading is a feminine occupation. In our chauvinistic society, if they once begin to think of reading as sissy, they're in real trouble" (73). Even though society has come a long way since 1979, his point is still a valid one and gives teachers something to think about. Listed below are additional ideas to consider when organizing a listening center.

Materials to Include

The following are some materials you may want to include in your listening center. Feel free to add or delete items as you feel is appropriate for your students.

- **Big Books and small books** along with matching prerecorded audiotapes
- **Audiotapes** of the teacher doing lessons with books in the classroom
- **Cassette player**
- **Headphones** (You may find that it is easier to forego the headphones and simply teach children how to listen to the tapes at an appropriate volume so that others are not disturbed.)
- **Blank cassette tapes** (School supply catalogs often sell inexpensive 15-minute tapes.)
- **Reseable bags** (Resealable bags are very helpful in keeping books with the accompanying tapes.)

Activities to Do

The following are some suggested activities for the listening center. Choose the activities that are most appropriate for your students.

Early and Emergent Readers

Students can listen to recordings of texts alone, with a partner, or in a small group. Some ideas for text recordings include the following:

- **Have parents, grandparents, the local fire chief, and other important individuals record themselves reading a text of their choice.**

- **Have various staff members (the principal, the secretary, the music teacher) record their favorite book.**

- **Tape yourself as you do a lesson.** Kids will hear modeled reading, as well as having another opportunity to respond to the questions you ask.

- **Tape record your students singing or reading** and provide the lyrics or text for them to follow along.

- **Let students earn the privilege of recording a favorite book on tape.** This is especially good for intermediate students who need to work on practicing fluency—they can practice a book, record it with sound effects, and then donate it to a primary classroom. This also provides the teacher with a valuable assessment tool documenting that student's reading.

Note: *When recording, record the text over and over again on the tape so students do not have to rewind it constantly.*

Transitional and Fluent Readers

Teach children how to create and record new songs linked to content area information by changing the words to familiar tunes (e.g., to the tune of "Row, Row, Row Your Boat," sing the Christopher Columbus song "Sail, sail, sail your ship. Sail it night and day. Look for land, look for land, all along the way"). You can also encourage children to create their own tunes, raps, etc. with lyrics matching content area studies. This is a great study tool for all students.

> ## Efficiency and Effectiveness Task
>
> **Choose one center from the previous suggestions.** Choose two activities from the center to introduce to your students. The following week, introduce two more. Once you have five to six activities, choose another center and begin introducing activities. Once you have all your centers in place, slowly add additional activities to each center.

Appendix

CONTENTS

How Does the Classroom Feel? 122

How Does the Classroom Look? 123

How Does the Classroom Sound? 124

Peer Questions 125

Alphabet Chart 126

What Is On Your Walls? 127

AM To Do List 128

PM To Do List 129

Small Reading Group Notes 130

I'm Learning To . . . / I Can 131

Emergent Reading Checklist 132

Early Reading Checklist 133

Fluent Reading Checklist 134

Continuum of Written Language
    Development 135

Continuum of Written Language
    Development 136

Checklist for Reading Assessment 137

Teaching Routines Checklist 138

Center Icons 139

Card Templates 142

Center Group Icons 143

Contract 1 144

Contract 2 145

Contract 3 146

Poem 1 147

Poem 2 148

Using Pictures to Prompt Writing 149

How Does the Classroom Feel?

Teacher: _____

Grade Level: _____ School Year: _____ Number of Students: _____

✔ Do I feel comfortable as I enter?

✔ Do I get a peaceful sense of order, or am I overwhelmed by a sense of chaos?

✔ Is this a place where I would enjoy spending six (give or take) hours a day? Would I want to learn here? Could I learn here?

✔ What appears to be important in this room?

How Does the Classroom Look?

Teacher:

Grade Level: School Year: Number of Students:

✔ Is there a teacher's desk? If so, where is it? How and when is it used?

✔ How are the student desks or tables organized?

✔ Are there logical pathways for movement?

✔ Is there a floor space large enough for the whole group to sit comfortably?

✔ Is there some place for children to work quietly?

✔ Are materials well organized and accessible?

✔ Is there an overabundance of workbooks and worksheets?

✔ Is there a lot of unnecessary clutter?

✔ Is there a word wall? What is on it? How is it being used? (This should be empty initially, and grow as the year goes on.)

✔ Is there a letter line? What is on it? How is it used?

✔ What else is on the walls?

✔ Is there a classroom library? How is it organized?

✔ Is there a big-book stand for shared reading?

✔ Are there writing spaces available for modeling?

✔ Do students have a sense of how the environment has been organized?

How Does the Classroom Sound?

Teacher:

Grade Level: School Year: Number of Students:

✔ Whose voices do I hear? What are they saying?

✔ How effectively can the teacher get students' attention?

Peer Questions

Teacher: _____   Date _____

Have your peer answer or ask yourself the following questions:

- Where does the teacher position him- or herself for instruction?

- Is there absolute silence, except for when the teacher is speaking or asking a question?

- Is there an imposing feeling of control?

- Does the teacher go to the children or do the children have to go to the teacher?

- If the children go to the teacher, is there a long line of children constantly seeking help or approval?

- Is covering the content, regardless of student needs, an overshadowing characteristic?

- Physically, how are things organized?

- How does the teacher convey that books and reading are important? Are books easily accessible to students?

- How does the teacher honor children's work? Is the work visible?

- Do learners appear to be self-motivated and independent?

Alphabet Chart

Aa Bb Cc Dd

Ee Ff Gg Hh

Ii Jj Kk Ll

Mm Nn Oo Pp

Qq Rr Ss Tt

Uu Vv Ww Xx

Yy Zz Aa Bb Cc Dd Ee Ff Gg Hh Ii
Jj Kk Ll Mm Nn Oo Pp Qq Rr
Ss Tt Uu Vv Ww Xx Yy Zz

Adapted for I Teach Phonics...And I Love It! *by Lisa Dellamora ©1997. Reprinted with permission.*

What Is On Your Walls?

Fill out the following chart. As you go through your day, circle the items your students use or attend to regularly. Star the items you model the use of. After about a week, review your list and decide which materials on your walls are valuable instructional materials and which need to go.

Items I Purchased	Things I Made

Things I Made With My Students	Things My Students Made

AM To Do List

Monday	Tuesday	Wednesday	Thursday	Friday
DATE	DATE	DATE	DATE	DATE
8:30	8:30	8:30	8:30	8:30
8:45	8:45	8:45	8:45	8:45
9:00	9:00	9:00	9:00	9:00
9:15	9:15	9:15	9:15	9:15
9:30	9:30	9:30	9:30	9:30
9:45	9:45	9:45	9:45	9:45
10:00	10:00	10:00	10:00	10:00
10:15	10:15	10:15	10:15	10:15
10:30	10:30	10:30	10:30	10:30
10:45	10:45	10:45	10:45	10:45
11:00	11:00	11:00	11:00	11:00
11:15	11:15	11:15	11:15	11:15
11:30	11:30	11:30	11:30	11:30
11:45	11:45	11:45	11:45	11:45
12:00	12:00	12:00	12:00	12:00

PM To Do List

Monday	Tuesday	Wednesday	Thursday	Friday
DATE	DATE	DATE	DATE	DATE
11:45	11:45	11:45	11:45	11:45
12:00	12:00	12:00	12:00	12:00
12:15	12:15	12:15	12:15	12:15
12:30	12:30	12:30	12:30	12:30
12:45	12:45	12:45	12:45	12:45
1:00	1:00	1:00	1:00	1:00
1:15	1:15	1:15	1:15	1:15
1:30	1:30	1:30	1:30	1:30
1:45	1:45	1:45	1:45	1:45
2:00	2:00	2:00	2:00	2:00
2:15	2:15	2:15	2:15	2:15
2:30	2:30	2:30	2:30	2:30
2:45	2:45	2:45	2:45	2:45
3:00	3:00	3:00	3:00	3:00
3:15	3:15	3:15	3:15	3:15

Small Reading Group Notes

Lesson plans for the week of: _____ to _____ . Group: _____

Monday	Tuesday	Wednesday	Thursday	Friday
Text:	Text:	Text:	Text:	Text:
Planned Teaching Points:	Planned Teaching Points:	Planned Teaching Points:	Planned Teaching Points:	Planned Teaching Points:
Notes:	Notes:	Notes:	Notes:	Notes:

Anecdotal notes on students:

Student:	Student:	Student:	Student:	Student:

I'm Learning To . . . / I Can . . .

Name _____

I'm learning to . . .	I can . . .

Emergent Reading Checklist

Name _____ Grade _____ Age _____

Knowledge of print behavior and strategies	Comments	Date
Enjoys listening to stories		
Uses reading-like behavior to approximate book language		
Uses meaning of the story to make predictions		
Chooses to read from various sources		
Notices and reads environmental print		
Can sit for a time and read a book		
Participates confidently in shared reading		
Retells stories and rhymes		
Likes to write		
Understands that writers use letter symbols to construct meaning		
Can show the front cover of book		
Understands that the print carries the message		
Uses pictures as clues to the story line		
Knows where to start reading the text		
Knows where to stop reading the text		
Knows which way to go, L–R, and return		
Knows which way to go, top to bottom		
Can point and match 1:1 as teacher reads		
Knows sounds and names of a few letters		
Can indicate and recognize few/some words		
Can indicate the space between the words		
Understands the difference between letters and words		
Can recognize some high-frequency words both in and out of context		
Can write some high-frequency words independently		

From *Guided Reading Workshop* ©2002 Rigby. Reprinted with permission.

Early Reading Checklist

Name _____ Grade _____ Age _____

Knowledge of print behavior and strategies	Comments	Date
Enjoys listening to stories		
Is confident about sharing feelings about books		
Chooses to read independently		
Chooses to explore unfamiliar resources		
Developing ability to retell longer stories in sequence		
Developing ability to recall facts in informational books		
Participates confidently in shared reading		
Participates confidently in shared writing		
More reliant on visual cues than picture cues		
Beginning to integrate strategies to cross-check when constructing meaning:		
1. checks predictions by looking at letters and words		
2. rereads to check meaning		
3. notices mismatches and works on them		
4. brings own knowledge of oral and written language to reading		
Beginning to check graphophonic information as a means of confirming prediction		
Expects to get meaning from text		
Reads word-by-word and points with finger/voice		
Recognizes and builds a vocabulary of sight words		
Can write and spell correctly some high-frequency words		
Begins to identify misspelled words in own writing		
Takes responsibility for selecting words for personal spelling lists		
Writes with confidence and enthusiasm		
Beginning to take initiative for responding creatively to books		
Developing ability to identify approximations in personal writing		

From *Guided Reading Workshop* ©2002 Rigby. Reprinted with permission.

Fluent Reading Checklist

Name _____ Grade _____ Age _____

Knowledge of print behavior and strategies	Comments	Date
Enjoys listening to longer stories		
Enjoys listening to chapter-book stories as well as picture books		
Reads silently for leisure, pleasure, and information		
Chooses to read independently from an increasing variety of genres for a variety of purposes		
Chooses to explore unfamiliar resources		
Reads chapter books and nonfiction informational texts of particular interest		
Expects to have independent control of first reading of an unseen text and demonstrates confidence when doing so		
Emergent and early reading strategies are secure and habituated		
Integrates and crosschecks language cues effectively		
Monitors and checks own reading with confidence		
Becomes more critical and reflective about the message and information in text		
Expects challenges—demonstrates strategies for handling them		
Is able to summarize information		
Proofreads writing and shows increased knowledge of systems for conventional spellings		
Demonstrates a growing understanding of writing in different registers for different purposes		
Is able to locate information in index		
Contributes effectively in shared writing		
Confident independent reader, ready to go on reading to learn and using reading and writing as tools for learning		

From *Guided Reading Workshop* ©2002 Rigby. Reprinted with permission.

Continuum of Written Language Development

Name _____ Grade _____ Age _____

Date entries. Note progress, any comments on child's samples.

	Date of Entry			Comments
Chooses own topics				
Makes lists, notes, and jots down ideas				
Demonstrates topic knowledge				
Explains ideas clearly				
Maintains sequence				
Attempts various writing forms:				
Narrative				
Personal narrative				
Explanation				
Recount				
Report				
Letter				
Diary				
Instructions				
Captions				
Rhymes				
Vocabulary:				
Uses effective adjectives/adverbs				
Uses comparisons (metaphors, similes)				
Tries out new vocabulary				
Spelling:				
Many close approximations				
Marks approximations for checking				
More correct spelling than [can't read copy]				
Uses correct word endings				
Sentence structure:				
Partially correct sentences				
Complete grammatical sentences (He ran down the road.)				
Maintenance of tense in short, straightforward pieces				
Compound sentences (two sentences linked by "and," "but," "or")				

From *Guided Reading Workshop* ©2002 Rigby. Reprinted with permission.

Continuum of Written Language Development

Name _____   Grade _____   Age _____

Date entries. Note progress, any comments on child's samples.

	Date of Entry			Comments
Adventurous sentences which relate ideas and information in complex ways but are not always grammatically correct				
Adventurous and grammatically correct sentences				
Varied sentence beginnings				
Sentences that use phrases/lists of words, etc.				
Sentences that use alliteration, onomatopoeia, and other figures of speech				
Sentences that use special effects to build atmosphere				
Punctuation:				
Awareness of periods, capitals in signal sentences				
Competent use of periods, capitals in signal sentences				
Awareness of commas, exclamation marks, question marks				
Competent use of commas, exclamation and question marks				
Awareness of dialogue, quotation marks				
Competent use of dialogue, quotation marks				
Starting to use paragraphs				
Using paragraphs				
Editing skills:				
Uses arrows, lines, insertions, etc.				
Crosses out and rewrites				
Tries out spelling in several ways				
Circles things to check				
Rereads to see how it sounds				
Using Word Processors:				
Find the appropriate letters, spaces, capitals, etc.				
Uses editing keys				
Deletions				
Corrections				
Insertions				
Spell check				
Manipulates the print on screen				
Prints/saves				

From *Guided Reading Workshop* ©2002 Rigby. Reprinted with permission.

Checklist for Reading Assessment

Name _____   Age _____

Grade _____   First Language _____   Second Language _____

Assessment Rubric: 0 = not applicable   1 = rarely   2 = sometimes   3 = often

Observation	Quarter				Comments
	1	**2**	**3**	**4**	
Chooses appropriate reading material					
Reads a variety of reading genres					
Can read for a length of time					
Predicts story line					
Independently chooses to read					
Attempts to self-correct errors					
Uses appropriate phonetic strategies					
Has a self-monitoring mechanism					
Uses book language to express understanding					
Uses the library					
Can retell a story					
Can summarize a story					
Uses past experience to relate to story					
Uses a variety of ways to extend reading					

Teaching Routines Checklist

Teaching Routines	Routine	Date Introduced	Date Revisited
Using materials			
Managing noise levels			
Getting help			
Getting student's attention			
Working inside the classroom (alone and with others)			
Working outside the classroom			

Center Icons

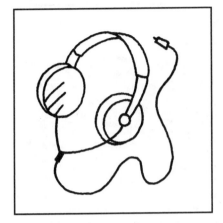

Listening Center

Poetry Center

Classroom Library

Handwriting/ Penmanship Center

Writing Center

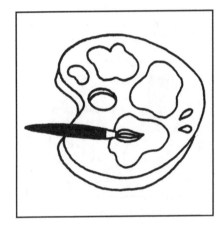

Art Library

Word Zone

Read the Room

Computer

Center Icons *(continued)*

Book Boxes

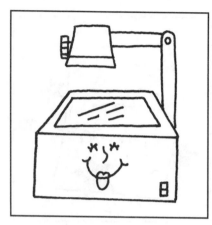

Overhead Projector

Alphabet Center

Science

Show and Tell

Puzzles

Pocket Chart

Music

Dramatic Play

Center Icons *(continued)*

Mathematics **Housekeeping** **Blocks**

Choice

Card Templates

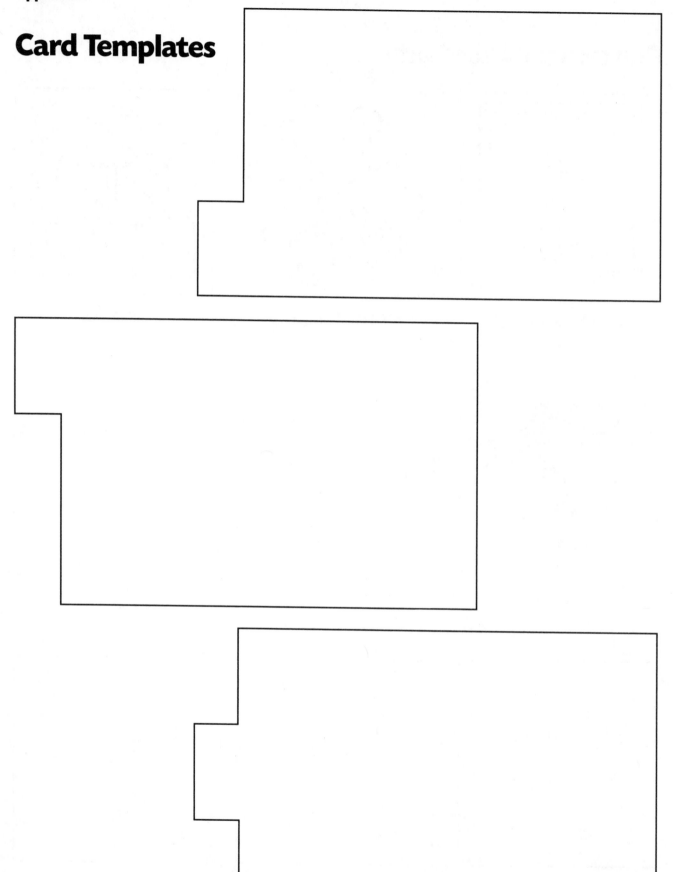

Center Group Icons

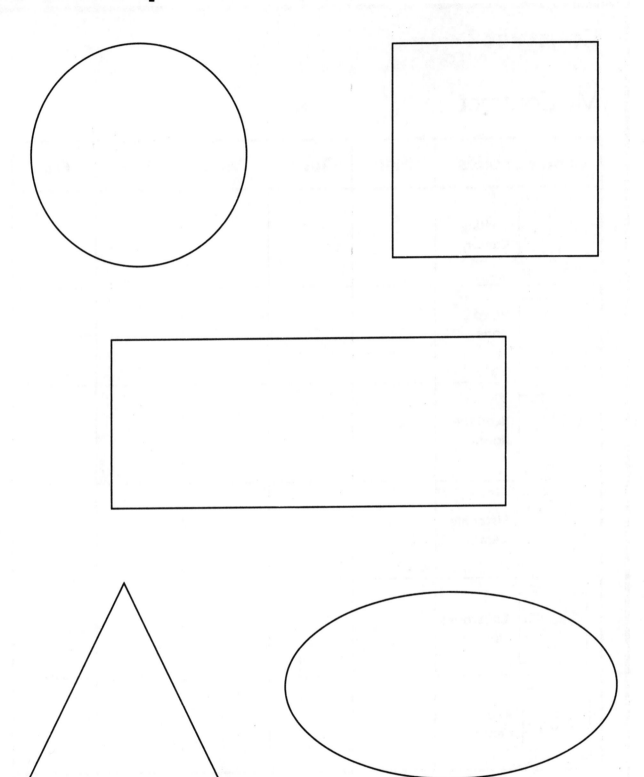

Contract 1

My Contract

Name _____

Center Choices	Mon.	Tues.	Wed.	Thurs.	Fri.
Writing Center					
Word Zone					
Read the Room					
Listening Center					
Classroom Library					
Art Center					

Write about what you learned on the back of your contract at the end of the week.

Adapted from *Rigby Literacy*. © 2000 Rigby. Reprinted with permission.

Contract 2

My Contract
Name _____

Center Choices	Mon.	Tues.	Wed.	Thurs.	Fri.
Writing Center					
Word Zone					
Read the Room					
Listening Center					
Classroom Library					
Art Center					
Overhead					

Write about what you learned on the back of your contract at the end of the week.

Adapted from *Rigby Literacy*. © 2000 Rigby. Reprinted with permission.

Contract 3

Name _____ Week of _____

Center Choices	Mon.	Tues.	Wed.	Thurs.	Fri.
Classroom Library					
Word Zone					
Computer Center					
Art Center					
Writing Center					
Read the Room					
Listening Center					

Did you make good decisions this week? _____

Write about what you learned this week. _____

_____

_____

Parent Signature _____

Comments _____

Adapted from *Rigby Literacy*. © 2000 Rigby. Reprinted with permission.

Poem 1

The sun is yellow.
The sun is bright.
It shines all day,
But not at night.

Adapted for *I Teach Phonics…And I Love It!* by Lisa Dellamora ©1997. Reprinted with permission.

Poem 2

The queen's pet duck said,
"Quack! Quack! Quack!"

"Be quiet!" she yelled,
"or I'll take you back!"

Adapted for *I Teach Phonics…And I Love It!* by Lisa Dellamora ©1997. Reprinted with permission.

Using Pictures To Prompt Writing

Note the opportunities for differentiating instruction by ability level or instructional focus. Be sure to introduce options over time, and precede each task with plenty of discussion and modeling.

Labels
Identify items in the picture, stretch out the words, and record the sounds.

Using Adjectives
Identify items in the picture, and label them using one or more describing words.

Snowballs
Identify an item in the picture and build a growing list, describing the object.

```
dog
small dog
small furry dog
small furry brown dog
```

Story Writing

1. Describe what is happening in the picture.

   The boy is walking his dog.

2. Add names and other details to make your story more interesting.

   John is walking his dog Spot. Spot likes to go for walks in the park.

3. Add dialogue to the story.

   "Come on, Spot!" yelled John. "Let's go for a walk..."

4. Write what happened before and/or after, as well as during the picture.

   The blizzard lasted for three days! Finally John's mother let him go outside. "Whoopee!" yelled John...

5. "This reminds me of ... " (Instead of writing about the picture, write the story it makes you think of from your own experiences.)

   "Brandy!" said my mom. "Brandy McMuffin of Hayden is what we'll call her."

Odds and Ends

1. Write lists related to the picture. (*i.e. things you wear when it's cold, pets, pet names, etc.*)

2. What kinds of things might you hear people saying here?

3. Write a letter to or from one of the people in the picture.

Bibliography

Allington, Richard. 2001. *What really matters for struggling readers: Designing researched-based programs.* New York: Addison Wesley Longman.

Beatles. 1967. *I get by with a little help from my friends.* Capitol Records.

Bickart, Toni S., Jablon, Judy R., & Dodge, Trister, Diane. 1999. *Building the primary classroom: A complete guide to teaching and learning.* Washington, DC: Teaching Strategties.

Bruner, Jerome. 1960. *The process of education.* Cambridge, MA: Harvard University Press.

Caine, Renate Nummela, & Caine, Geoffrey. 1994. *Making connections: Teaching and the human brain.* Menlo Park, CA: Addison-Wesley.

1997. *Education on the edge of possibility.* Alexandria, VA: Association for Supervision and Curriculum Development.

Calkins, Lucy. 1999. *Re-imagining the reading/writing workshop.* Portsmouth, NH: Heinemann Workshops.

Calkins, Lucy, Montgomery, Kate, & Santman, Donna. 1998. *A teacher's guide to standardized reading tests: Knowledge is power.* Portsmouth, NH: Heinemann.

Cambourne, Brian. 1988. *The whole story.* Auckland, New Zealand: Ashton Scholastic.

Charles, C. M. 1998. *Building classroom discipline.* New York: Longman.

Clay, Marie. 1993. *An observation survey.* Portsmouth, NH: Heinemann.

Covey, Stephen R. 1989. *The seven habits of highly effective people.* New York, NY: Simon and Schuster.

Cunningham, Patricia M. 1995. *Phonics the use: Words for reading and writing.* New York: HarperCollins College Publishers.

Dangerous Minds. 1995. Produced by Don Simpson and Jerry Bruckheimer. Directed by John N. Smith. 99 minutes. Buena Vista Entertainment. Videocassette.

Danielson, Charlotte. 1996. *Enhancing professional practice: A framework for teaching.* Alexandria, VA: Association for Supervision and Curriculum Development.

Dellamora, Lisa. 1997. *I teach phonics...And I love it!!!* Barrington, IL: Stella's Stuff.

Dorn, Linda J., French, Cathy, & Jones, Tammy. 1998. *Apprenticeship in literacy: Transitions across reading and writing.* York, ME: Stenhouse Publishers.

Education Department of South Australia. 1991. *Assessment of writing and reading inservice teacher education: Literacy asessment in practice: R-7 language arts.* Adelaide: Author.

Elting, Mary. 1980. *Q is for duck.* New York: Houghton Mifflin Company.

Everston, Carolyn M., Emmer, Edmond T., & Worsham, Murray. E. 2003. *Classroom management for elementary teachers.* Boston, MA: Allyn and Bacon.

Fisher, Bobbi. 1991. *Joyful learning.* Portsmouth, NH: Heinemann.

Forester, Anne, & Reinhard, Margaret. 1994. *The teacher's way.* Winnipeg, Manitoba: Peguis Publishers.

Fountas, Irene C., & Pinnell, Gay Su. 1996. *Guided reading: Good first teaching for all children.* Portsmouth, NH: Heinemann.

Glasser, William. 1993. *The quality school teacher.* New York: HarperPerennial.

Graves, Donald. 1994. *A fresh look at writing.* Portsmouth, NH: Heinemann

Groeber, Joan. 2001. *Power of poetry.* Barrington, IL: Rigby.

Harste, Jerome C., Short, Kathy G., & Burke, Carolyn. 1988. *Creating classrooms for authors: The reading-writing connection.* Portsmouth, NH: Heinemann.

Hart, L. A. 1983. *Human brain, human learning.* New York: Longman.

Harvey, Stephanie, & Goudvis, Anne. 2000. *Strategies that work: Teaching comprehension to enhance understanding.* York, ME: Stenhouse Publishers.

Hill, Bonnie Campbell, Ruptic, Cynthia, & Norwick, Lisa. 1998. *Classroom based assessment.* Norwood, MA: Christopher-Gordon Publishers.

Hindley, Joanne. 1996. *In the company of children.* York, ME: Stenhouse Publishers.

Holdaway, Don. 1979. *The foundations of literacy.* Gosford, New South Wales: Ashton Scholastic.

Jensen, Eric. 1995. *Brain-based learning.* San Diego, CA: The Brain Store Publishing.

1998. *Teaching with the brain in Mind.* Alexandria, VA: Association for Supervision and Curriculum Development.

Kagan, Spencer. 1992. *Cooperative learning.* San Clemente, CA: Kagan.

Keene, Ellin Oliver, & Zimmermann, Susan. 1997. *Mosaic of thought.* Portsmouth, NH: Heinemann.

Kohn, Alfie. 1993. *Punished by rewards: The trouble with gold stars, incentive plans, A's, praise, and other bribes.* New York: Houghton Mifflin Company.

Kovalik, Susan J., & Olsen, Karen D. 2002. *Exceeding expectations: A user's guide to implementing brain research in the classroom.* Covington, WA: Susan Kovalik and Associates.

Martin, Bill. 1967. *Brown bear, brown bear, what do you see?* New York: Holt, Rinehart, and Winston.

Mooney, Margaret. 1990. *Reading to, with, and by children.* Katonah, NY: Richard C. Owen Publishers.

Nations, Susan, & Alonso, Mellissa. 2001. *Primary literacy centers: Making reading and writing stick!* Gainsville, FL: Maupin House.

Ohlihausen, Marliyn M., & Jepsin, Mary. 1992. Lessons from Goldilocks: Somebody's been choosing my books but I can make my own choices now! *The New Advocate, 5, 36.*

Platt, Robyn. 1996. *ELIC Facilitator Training,* Rigby Education: Barrington, IL.

Routman, Regie. 1999. *Conversations: Strategies for teaching, learning, and evaluating.* Portsmouth, NH: Heinemann.

Servis, Joan. 1999. *Celebrating the fourth.* Portsmouth, NH: Heinemann.

Seuss, Dr. 1963. *Dr. Seuss' abc.* New York: Random House.

Silverstein, Shel. 1964. *The giving tree.* New York: HarperCollins Publishers.

1974. *Where the sidewalk ends.* New York: HarperCollins Children's Books.

Shannon, George. 1996. *Tomorrow's alphabet.* New York: Scholastic.

Smith, Frank. 1985. *Reading without nonsense.* New York: Teachers College Press.

1986. *Insult to intelligence.* Portsmouth, NH: Heinemann.

Sylwester, Robert. 1998. *The downshifting dilemma: A commentary and proposal.* Seattle, WA: New Horizons for Learning.

Taberski, Sharon. 2000. *On solid ground.* Portsmouth, NH: Heinemann.

Van Allsburg, Chris. 1987. *The z was zapped.* New York: Houghton Mifflin Company.

Veatch, Jeanette. 1959. *Individualizing your reading program.* New York: Putnam.

Wagstaff, Janiel M. 1999. *Teaching reading and writing with word walls: Easy lessons and fresh ideas for creating interactive word walls that build literacy skills.* New York: Scholastic.

Wong, Harry. 1998. *The first days of school.* Mountain View, CA: Harry K. Wong Publications.